Restoring and Preserving Antiques

RESTORING AND PRESERVING ANTIQUES

by Frederic Taubes

Watson-Guptill Publications
New York

Contents

Other Books by Frederic Taubes

FOREWORD

In this book, I shall describe simple methods of restoring and preserving objects made of wood, marble, limestone, terracotta and related materials, whether ornamental or utilitarian. Moreover, I shall explain the techniques of gilding and silvering, as well as methods of treating bronze, brass, and copper. Cleaning, repairing, and preserving paintings will also be described in detail. Particular attention will be given to the reestablishment of appropriate patinas in case these have been lost.

I must mention that I am a painter by training. Only during the past twenty-five years have I learned the techniques described in this treatise. Although I had been collecting antiques for over four decades, I discovered the enormous gratification of restoring them after World War II, when I could resume traveling to the European continent. Since then, restoring antiques has become my principal and most rewarding hobby. All the technical processes described here are the result of actual experience. I have meticulously avoided quoting from dubious sources and making assertions based merely on hearsay.

These skills can be acquired by any layman who has a desire to work with his hands. Anyone—even without specialized training—who follows the directions given in this manual can expect good results. For notes about materials and tools which may be unfamiliar, see Chapter 8.

F. T., New York

INTRODUCTION

Works of art, decorative objects, and artifacts —both ancient and not so ancient—inevitably deteriorate with the passage of time. Some defects occur because of interior weakness or because an inappropriate material went into their making. Some suffer damage due to careless handling or accidents.

Painting, sculpture, and decorative objects

The requirements of restoration are quite different in paintings and in works conceived in three dimensions—sculpture, decorative carvings, etc. When a painting is damaged —that is, cracked, torn, or suffering some surface loss—even to a slight degree, it must be restored to a reasonable semblance of its original condition. Picture dealers and museums know this well; they will never show a painting in a state of deterioration. But this is not always so when we consider three dimensional works. We often hear a merchant of antiques state that a battered statue is in "original condition," meaning that it was never repaired. Thus, the unrepaired condition is supposed to represent a special value.

In my view, this attitude toward three dimensional objects lacks justification, for it means that any blind hazard that may have befallen a statue should remain irreversible, that whatever defaces its form is, ipso facto, sanctified. True, a battered head of great antiquity may be more attractive than an unscathed one—providing that the damages are minor and have occurred in the "right places." Fragments do hold a special fascination for us, for they galvanize the imagination and feed our feeling of nostalgia. (Of course, this particular reaction is characteristic of our own times and cannot be considered universally valid.) But if an armless or headless Greek or

11

Roman statue gratifies our esthetic sensibilities, the same cannot be said of a Renaissance or a Baroque object: just imagine Michelangelo's *David* minus his nose—we would all cry out for speedy rectification.

However, we can accept the general rule that certain types of statuary—and all objects that relate to architectural decor in some way—should not be restored to a point where they would look brand new. All three dimensional objects originated as part of an architectural setting, and it is expected that ancient architecture should look ancient, that it carries the marks of age, that it is endowed with a patina which only time—or the skillful hand and judicious mind of a restorer—can provide.

Fine versus applied art

In dealing with antiques—by which I simply mean objects of the past—a distinction is generally made between works of fine art and those of decorative or applied art. However, such a division is often problematic, because, until the machine age, the borderline between fine and applied art was far from distinct. Such borderlines have been instituted arbitrarily by modern "authorities."

Pre-machine age utilitarian objects do possess art ingredients of various kinds. We must look upon them as "artistic"—at least in various degrees. Just think of Leonardo's statement, made in his "job application," addressed to Lodovico Moro, Duke of Milan; among the various capabilities listed, he writes: "Furthermore, if required, I shall make mortars and cannons of beautiful and useful shape, such as were hitherto unknown." Indeed, if you ever saw the mighty cannon placed on the ground floor of the Sforza Palace in Milan, you must concede that it is a work of art. And

consider the early Flemish and French tapestries, Gothic carvings, facades of churches, ecclesiastical statuary—are they not works of art? In short, when dealing with art forms of the past, I would not be too concerned about the distinction normally made between applied and fine arts.

Furniture and other utilitarian objects

This book will devote considerable space to strictly utilitarian objects—furniture in the main. Let me emphasize that all repairs requiring expert carpentry must be left to the professional cabinet maker. Skills of that nature cannot be acquired by reading manuals, no matter how explicit. But finishes of all sorts—calling for the application of paints, patinas, varnishes, gilding, etc.—can surely be handled by amateurs who gather their information from such a text as this. Although the beginner will not approach his task with great dexterity, after some initial attempts he will attain an adequate degree of skill.

Finishing furniture can call for polishing; repairs of cracks, fissures, holes, and worm-eaten areas; repairs of damage to polychromy (paint); and sometimes gold leafing. These processes will be found in separate chapters on treatment of wood and gilding. In the case of what I will call "non-antiques," the total refinishing of inexpensive pieces of furniture is described in a separate chapter.

At this point, it may be of interest to remark on the changes in public taste. A generation or two ago, it would have been considered poor taste to restore gilding on antique furniture. Gilding had to be dim and lusterless. This is not so today, when gilding has to be burnished to a brilliant gloss to achieve the eye appeal to which the public has been conditioned.

A word of warning

Having played down the distinction between fine and applied art objects, it is obviously important to emphasize the distinction between objects of modest value and objects of great value. It should be apparent to the reader that the instructions in this book are *not* intended for the restoration of costly works of art, objects of museum quality, and other priceless pieces which really belong in the hands of a professional restorer or conservator. If the reader can afford to buy such pieces in the first place, he can certainly afford the additional investment in professional care.

If you have any reason to believe that an object—even if it comes from a dusty corner of your attic—has significant financial value, I urge you to have it appraised before laying a hand on it. If it does prove to be as valuable as you hoped, the home craftsman should undertake only the simplest repairs—those which you are confident you can handle—remembering that even a slight mistake can mean a major loss in the appraised value of the object.

In short, the instructions in this book are meant for the do-it-yourself craftsman who works with modest paintings, sculptures, or decorative objects which do not involve great financial risk. If you tremble as you work, fearful of making an irreparable error on an object which has cost you a great deal of money, the satisfaction of your craft will quickly evaporate. In fact, much of the pleasure of restoration is precisely to begin with an object of small value and then transform it into an object of greater value by the work of your own hands.

As you read on in this book, you will find that many of my demonstration projects trace this process of transformation. I sometimes begin with a scrap of furniture or decorative ware which has literally no value—which is totally unsaleable in its original battered condition—and then experience the delight of converting it into something which is very attractive.

Since few readers are likely to be in the financial bracket of the fashionable art or antique collector, and since it is unlikely that you will find priceless treasures in your attic or your basement, this book emphasizes methods which are most suitable for the restoration of simple objects which the amateur can approach without anxiety—and with full confidence that his work will increase rather than decrease their financial value.

The procedures described on the following pages are designed specifically for amateurs, not for the use of professional finishers. Although I am conversant with industrial techniques, it has been my experience that factory methods cannot be employed by the inexperienced. Hence, I am introducing procedures which should satisfy the amateur craftsman without lowering his standards.

1
TREATING WOOD

Sandpapering

Refinishing is likely to begin by smoothing the surface. The term sandpaper is obsolete. The papers used today for this purpose are prepared from flint (these are off white in color), garnet (red), aluminum oxide (brown), and silicon carbide, also referred to as carborundum (black). The last two possess the most abrasive qualities. Polishing should start with a comparatively coarse grade and then proceed to the finer papers.

Sandpapering should always follow the grain of the wood, and never cut across it. It is practical to wrap the paper around a wood block 2″ x 3″ x 4″, with a piece of felt glued to its working surface. Special sandpaper holders are also available and, of course, a vibrator is most efficient (Fig. 1). When you are treating moldings, the sandpaper can be wrapped around a dowel stick of appropriate thickness.

Abrasives also come in powder form. These should be mixed with water or oil (linseed or crude oil), and applied in paste form. For our purposes, two of these powders will be used: pumice and rotten-stone. The latter is the finest material there is for achieving mirror smooth surfaces.

Bleaching wood

The natural dark color of wood, as well as wood stained by dyes, can be bleached before applying fresh color. Certain pigments

FIGURE 1. *Electric (vibrator) sander.*

FIGURE 2. *Typical crack in wooden table top.*

FIGURE 3. *Cracked wooden table top partially filled with acrylic modeling paste (tinted to match wood tone) and touched up with oil colors to match grain.*

will resist the bleaching process, and therefore the surface of the wood may have to be sanded in order to deprive it of its coloring. There are a number of standard bleaches on the market. The one most generally used is known as Clorox. A more effective product combination is sold under the trade names Color Dissolvent, Decolorant, and Bleach Booster (see Chapter 8).

Before applying a bleach, the surface of the wood must first be freed from all old coatings: varnish, oil, wax, or whatever covers the natural surface. Paint remover will do a thorough job of cleaning, but it will also leave a residue of paraffin, which should be eliminated with painters' thinner or any petroleum solvent.

Next, for partial bleaching, apply one coat of Decolorant and allow it to dry for four hours. After four hours, apply a second coat if further bleaching is required. If residual chemical stains are still present, apply a final liberal coat of Bleach Booster to eradicate them. For *complete* bleaching, apply one coat of Color Dissolvent, follow with Decolorant after several minutes, and finish the job with Bleach Booster.

Repairs of wood surfaces

The problem of eliminating nail holes, cracks, splits, or other disfigurements in wood surfaces that have retained their natural texture is not as difficult as it may appear (Figs. 2 and 3).

If the cracks are not too wide, they can be best filled by using acrylic modeling paste (Liquitex). Its white color can be easily tinted by adding powdered pigment or acrylic paint. Should the paste become too stiff (if too much pigment is added), it can be thinned with a little acrylic painting medium. However, to serve as a filler, its consistency must be firm, like that of window putty.

A standard wood putty can be used for filling extra deep cracks. For applying the paste or putty, a palette knife should be used; its broad edge will produce a perfectly smooth surface and a polishing paper will make it mirror smooth. (Various knives are seen in Figs. 4 and 5.)

If the wood finish is non-glossy, the color of the putty should be modified to match that of the material under repair. For the common varieties of wood—such as pine, spruce, maple, birch, poplar, oak, chestnut, walnut, basswood, etc.—intermixtures of the following dry pigments, mixed with putty or modeling paste, will yield the needed colors: yellow ochre, raw and burnt siena, raw and burnt umber.

Repairs on glossy surfaces are more difficult because polished wood has a translucent quality which the colored filler cannot provide. Therefore, in such instances, our procedure will differ from that mentioned above.

The crack should be filled with white acrylic modeling paste to appear perfectly flush with the top surface; upon drying, the paste should be well polished. Next, alcohol soluble dyes of appropriate colors should be intermixed to the consistency of watercolor (usually, ochre, umber, and burnt siena will do) and these should be applied to the white modeling paste with a sable brush. Graining can be produced easily with this material. Upon drying, which takes but a few minutes, the color will appear matte and much lighter. Finally, an application of a fast drying varnish, such as Rockhard Finish Varnish, will deepen the color and produce a high gloss.

To repeat, acrylic modeling paste is suitable for filling in cracks and holes of insignificant width and depth, but not for large repairs because thick applications of the paste dry slowly and have a tendency to

FIGURE 4. *Palette knives for diverse operations.*

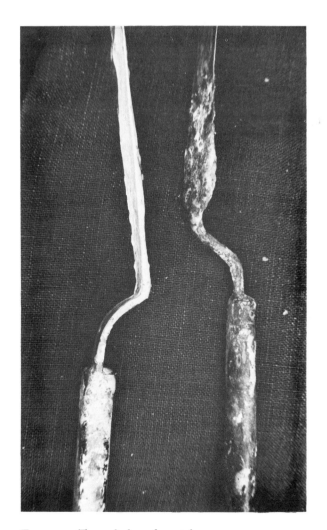

FIGURE 5. *Trowel shaped spatulas.*

fissure at the top surface. Therefore, for larger cracks, wood putty should be used in the deeper area of the crack and modeling paste on top. Plastic wood is not suitable for this purpose, because it does not provide a good ground for overpainting.

Three methods of coloring raw wood

Let us now take up the problem of raw wood coloring.

There are three categories of treatment: one which retains and exploits the natural texture (that is, the grain) of the wood; a second, which partly obscures the natural texture; and a third which conceals the texture entirely by overpainting.

Transparent finishes

Let us start with the first and simplest treatment—transparent coloring. Five different approaches can be considered here:

(1) *Wood stains* come in a large variety of colors. They are made of aniline dyes and their vehicles can be water, alcohol, oil, or a petroleum derivative. Some of the dyes have the tendency to bleed through the top finish, whether wax or varnish, hence they must be protected by a coat of shellac before waxing or varnishing. Most aniline stains become lighter when exposed to strong light, especially sunlight.

(2) *Acrylic paints,* because of their wide use, are preferable to dyes (or stains, as they are called). These paints are prepared from pigments and must be greatly diluted with water to become transparent. I am referring here to artists' colors (not to house paints) which come in tubes or jars. One can also mix any of the dry pigments with acrylic medium, which provides a certain amount of gloss, or with matte acrylic medium, which produces a non-glossy surface. However, on the absorbent surfaces of soft woods, all acrylic finishes will appear flat. To produce the desired transparency requisite for staining, water must be added to the acrylic paints as well as to the medium used as a binder for dry pigments. Both the dyes and the acrylics can be applied with a piece of rag or a brush.

(3) *Shellac* is another coloring substance— orange shellac or shellac tinted with an alcohol soluble dye. As a rule, shellac should be brushed on full strength as it comes from the can. When diluted with shellac thinner (denatured alcohol) its gloss will diminish and its color becomes lighter. However, in contrast to stains and acrylic paints, this ingredient will produce considerable gloss even on raw wood. Orange shellac will produce an "antique" effect on raw pine wood, but to conjure up an antique appearance, artificial aging of freshly cut pine boards is necessary before the application of shellac. This can best be done with the following method of coloring.

(4) *Pigment and turpentine.* Here the chosen dry pigment (such as light ochre, raw and burnt siena, raw and burnt umber) should simply be dispersed in turpentine. The more turpentine is used, the weaker the color effect will be. The turpentine-pigment mixture should be rubbed into the texture of the wood with a piece of rag rather than a brush. Once dry, the colors imbedded in the grain will not come off. As a matter of fact, their removal becomes impossible unless the wood is thoroughly sanded.

(5) *Pigment and wax.* First raw beeswax (bleached or unbleached) is turned into a paste. To do this, place a piece of wax, plus three times its weight in turpentine, in a double boiler and heat until the solution is fully blended. This paste can be mixed with dry pigments for coloring. One can

also use any good commercial paste or liquid wax, mixed with dry pigment, for the same purpose.

If varnish instead of turpentine is mixed with the beeswax, a more lustrous surface will be produced. This wax-resin compound, as it is called, will be described below. Hardwoods are particularly suitable for this type of coloring, but unlike finishes produced with turpentine, wax will leave a sheen on the surface. Depending on the nature of the wax and the surface of the wood (that is, the degree of its smoothness and hardness), semi-glossy or high gloss finishes can be obtained. A smooth, hardwood surface colored with a wax-resin compound will acquire a polish of maximum luster. Not only pigments, but a thick solution of asphaltum can be added to the wax-resin paste; glowing, brownish tones can be obtained in this manner.

Wax-resin compounds

This compound combines beeswax and damar varnish or Carnauba wax and copal varnish; both can receive a 5% addition of Venice turpentine to improve handling qualities. The beeswax-damar compound does not solidify to as hard a surface as the Carnauba-copal formulation; on seriously weakened wooden objects, one may assume that the harder blend gives more durable protection.

For the soft wax-resin compound, 1 oz. beeswax and 4 oz. damar varnish are heated in a double boiler until blended.

The hard compound is begun by splintering and pulverizing the Carnauba wax with a knife. An ounce of wax is then placed in an aluminum container and melted on a hot plate; when it liquefies, a few teaspoons of copal varnish should be added and stirred until the two components blend (too much cold varnish will make the mixture congeal). Now more copal varnish is poured in slowly until the ratio is 1 oz. wax to 6 oz. varnish.

The congealed paste should be applied thinly with a clean, lint-free cloth and allowed to solidify for about thirty minutes before polishing.

It must be mentioned that this formula employs only the copal varnish produced by Permanent Pigments of Cincinnati, Ohio. Because of the variations in the material, other varnishes designated as "copal" may be unsuitable for this purpose.

Marginal methods of coloring wood

Inky, bluish effects, ranging from a light gray to the darkest black, can be achieved by using a solution of iron sulphate (or iron chloride or ferric nitrate) and tannic acid. These should be dissolved in water and intermixed in any desirable concentration.

Colors ranging from light brown to jet black can be produced on coarse-grained hardwood, such as oak or chestnut, by scorching it with a propane torch (Fig. 6), a Bunsen burner (Fig. 7), or an ordinary gas flame. Depending on the length of the exposure to the flame, any desirable color within the indicated range can be obtained. When sanded and polished with steel wool, surfaces treated in this manner will show a considerable gloss.

Choosing the right method

As I have stated, some of these processes of coloring provide flat (matte) surfaces and some produce more or less glossy surfaces. Hence, before choosing one process over another, the nature of the object and its final appearance must be considered. Naturally, some of these finishes can be modified by further treatment: the matte acrylic finish on a stained surface can be

FIGURE 6. *Propane torch.*

FIGURE 7. *Bunsen burner.*

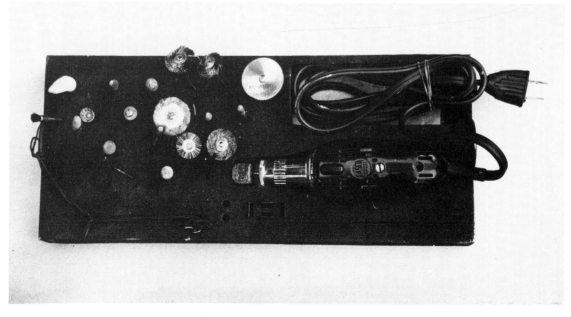

FIGURE 8. *Electric tool with various attachments for woodworking.*

waxed for further protection; the pigment and turpentine finish can be shellacked or waxed; and various surfaces can be enriched by the glossy finishes I will describe next. In short, finishes can be *combined* to suit your needs.

Glossy finishes

Recipes for glossy finishes of wood are many, and there are numerous commercial materials available on the market. I have had experience with only a few, although there can be little doubt that an unsatisfactory commercial product is rare today—the competition in this field is too keen to allow this to happen. Yet, the methods recommended here have been evolved in my own practice and have the advantage of being simple, foolproof, and well adapted to the needs of the amateur craftsman.

When a glossy wood surface appears to be desirable, you may be dealing with: (1) an untreated surface; (2) a finish that has become lackluster; (3) a glossy finish that needs restoration.

(1) *Untreated wood.* The porosity of the material must first be dealt with. Some woods are more, some less, porous. A well seasoned hardwood will receive a high polish when treated with wax alone, but a sealer must normally be used on soft wood surfaces. There are several sealers on the market, serving this purpose, but we shall use acrylic gel. Rubbed into the surface with a piece of cheesecloth (or other lint-free material), it dries almost instantly.

Now, on a fine object made of wood, we may not wish to seal only the top surface; we may prefer a refined procedure referred to as French polish. We shall require two flat dishes for this, one containing shellac, the other linseed oil or common machine oil. A piece of cloth, folded into a pad, should be first dipped into the oil, then into the

shellac, and the mixture should be rubbed into the wood surface for a few minutes. Or first linseed oil alone can be rubbed into the surface with the cloth pad, followed by an application of shellac, rubbed into the surface with the same pad. This must be repeated several times, and the surface thus treated must be allowed to dry overnight. The next day (unless the wood is close grained) the surface will appear rather flat, in which case the French polish should be continued, until the gloss becomes permanent, or the surface could be waxed repeatedly with resin-wax compound for final protection.

(2) *Lackluster finish.* When we are dealing with a surface which was once treated, but now shows age and has become largely nonabsorbent, one application of French polish may be sufficient. Final waxing should follow.

(3) *Glossy but blemished finish.* A well polished surface that requires improvement, usually because of some blemishes that may mar its gloss, should merely be waxed. Wax-resin paste if used as furniture polish, can be made to flow more easily when compounded with a small addition (about 5%) of Venice turpentine. To incorporate this ingredient into the paste, both components should be liquefied in a water bath or double boiler, and then mixed together.

These glossy finishes can, of course, be applied over wood stain, acrylic paints, or turpentine and pigment.

18th century finish

In addition to the instructions given above, I should like to mention that the exquisite finish we know on 18th century fine furniture was achieved by first treating the raw wood with many applications of linseed oil (boiled linseed oil thinned with a little turpentine for better penetration), allowing each coat to dry well before proceeding with the next. (To speed up drying, we could add cobalt dryer in the amount of 2% to the oil.) Next, French polish was used as described, followed by repeated waxing.

Of course, between applications—whether linseed oil or French polish—a fine abrasive (polishing paper, pumice, and finally rottenstone) must be used to render the surface mirror-smooth.

A hand rubbed finish is laborious, of course, and therefore is rarely used commercially today. Instead, synthetic resin spray finishes have been generally adopted. Of course, the layman will not own a complex spraying apparatus, but he can avail himself of the Krylon spray or Jet-Spray Lacquer sold in aerosol cans—the same material used as a fixative for drawings. It is not easy to produce a perfectly even sheen in this manner on a larger surface. However, once applied, the synthetic surface coating, which dries almost instantly, lends itself to buffing, which intensifies and unifies its gloss. An electric tool with a buffing attachment (Fig. 8) or the vibrator (Fig. 1), covered with felt only, will greatly facilitate this task.

The sprayed surface can also be treated with the finest steel wool, in which case it will acquire a satiny sheen.

When waxed (preferably with wax-resin compound), the surface gloss and appearance will hardly differ from that produced by the classic oil-shellac method. I must quickly add, however, that my own inclination is to follow the traditional polishing procedure. But I confess that I am not in a position to compare an 18th century marquetry cabinet, in its original oil-shellac polish, with one sporting a synthetic resin finish; hence my preference may rest on ingrained conservatism.

Semi-opaque finishes

In the preceding pages I have described finishes that do not conceal the wood grain. Other finishes may partially cover the texture. The paint used for this purpose must be thin and light colored; it is then called a patina. But whatever its tone, the the wood suitable for this treatment must be darker than the covering tone and possess an open (that is, coarse) grain. Oak or chestnut have this characteristic.

The patina really can have only one color: a warm or a cold gray, produced most often from burnt or raw umber and white. For white, we shall use acrylic gesso (I recommend Liquitex) thinned with three parts of water; for the coloring matter, mix dry umber pigment with it. Why acrylic gesso? Simply because it becomes water-insoluble when dry; hence it need not be protected like traditional gesso. The use of dry pigments (instead of prepared acrylic colors) is desirable because the minute particles do not completely disperse in the liquid, and will enrich the color when the dry surface is finally subjected to sand-papering and polishing with steel wool.

To apply the patina, proceed as follows. Cover the entire surface with it, using a stiff utility brush, and working the liquid thoroughly into the wood texture. While still wet, rub the patina off the surface with a cloth, so as to allow the gray color to remain only in the grain of the wood (Fig. 9). Upon drying, sandpaper or rub the surface lightly with steel wool to obtain a high gloss. Of course, waxing will always add luster and additional protection.

Thus far, I have been describing a patina produced from a thin application of wet paint on a coarse or open grain surface. However, on close grain woods, dry pigment can be used for this purpose with great advantage. I have treated only black surfaces in this manner, but it is evident that dark colors other than black could be treated. On black, three pigments seem to produce the most pleasant effects: raw green earth, chalk, and rottenstone.

Any of these pigments (as well as others, if desired) can be used in the following manner. First, dark acrylic paint should be sparingly rubbed into the surface; it is best to use a piece of rag for this purpose. Then, before the paint is completely absorbed by the wood (before it is dry), the chosen pigment should be brushed lightly onto the surface and then forced into the grain by rubbing with a piece of cloth. This rubbing can be done on an almost dry surface; in the latter case, the color obtained will be more uniform. Such treatment will preserve the native characteristic (that is, the texture) of the wood (Figs. 10 and 11). Should a gloss appear desirable, sandpaper with fine emery cloth. Waxing, however, would *undo* the effect.

Opaque finishes

It goes without saying that opaque paint, whatever its nature, will entirely hide the wood grain; hence, the wood's native characteristics are immaterial. Readers who are familiar with antique objects that possess painted surfaces must have noticed that these often show blotches or discolorations of one kind or another; these are marks of distinction, not disfigurations. However, should the original paint actually have peeled off in spots, or become defaced, the surface will require restoration and antiquing.

Now we may again hear the objection that this is a "falsification of the original object." It is my contention, however, that if the "falsification" improves the appearance of the object, we should welcome it. Let

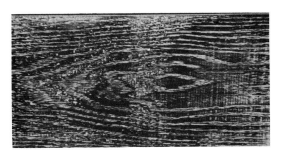

FIGURE 9. *Oak panel was darkened with acrylic color; gray patina (greatly thinned acrylic gesso and dry umber pigment) was rubbed into wood grain.*

FIGURE 10. *Wood panel was covered with black acrylic paint; raw green earth pigment was brushed onto slightly moist surface, then rubbed in with cloth.*

FIGURE 11. *Mahogany base was covered with black acrylic paint; rottenstone was rubbed into declivities of dry surface.*

FIGURE 12. *Light gray acrylic gesso foundation was coated with thin wash of black acrylic color, lifted here and there, while wet, with paper towel.*

FIGURE 13. *Light gray acrylic gesso foundation was glazed with phthalocyanine green and burnt siena. Wet acrylic glaze was textured with cheesecloth. Round sable brush was used to lift glaze, thus simulating marble veining.*

us remember that most, if not all, of the old master paintings and statues we see in museums had to undergo restorations of every kind; they are not entirely in their original condition.

Gesso surfacing

We may safely assume that the opaque surface coating of an antique object was made of gesso——a mixture of glue and whiting—the traditional material underlying most polychrome (colored) finishes. However, because the newer product possesses superior qualities, we shall most often employ the acrylic gesso (preferably Liquitex), not the traditional one.

However, in certain situations which I will discuss later, traditional gesso is necessary. To prepare this ancient recipe, soak 1 oz. powdered rabbit skin glue or hide glue overnight in 1 pt. water. By morning it will form a weak gel, which can be liquefied by heating (not boiling) in a double boiler. Add enough whiting to form a creamy solution. To increase opacity, add titanium white dry pigment to the whiting in a ratio of 1:4. The gesso will congeal as it cools, so keep it warm in the double boiler as you work. Add a few drops of phenol (carbolic acid) or store extra gesso or glue size in the refrigerator to retard spoilage.

Traditional gesso can be smoothed by sanding. But one cannot easily sandpaper the brush marks left by the harder acrylic gesso. The acrylic material is quite thick as it comes from the can and must be thinned with water to a more fluid state so its film will no longer retain brush marks. The wood surface will need three or four applications of thin gesso. However, there is a way to produce a smooth surface using a thicker solution: while it is still wet, brush the gessoed surface lightly with water. Of course, only a soft hair brush should be used for this purpose and sandpapering should proceed as soon as the surface becomes dry to the touch. A fine sandpaper and, whenever possible, an electric sander should be used for this purpose.

If a colored ground is needed, instead of mixing the white gesso with acrylic paints, I prefer to add a dry pigment which disperses easily in the gesso. However, one should be aware that because of its titanium white base, the tinting power of this gesso is enormous. In consequence, a great amount of colored pigment will be needed to overcome the strength of the white. Therefore, if you require a rather dark gesso, it is best to prepare your own, using whiting as its sole white pigment; whiting is weak in tinting strength and will not overwhelm the dark pigment. The whiting can be mixed either with acrylic polymer medium, or a glue size may serve as its binder (standard solution: 1 oz. glue, 1 pt. water kept warm in a double boiler as you add the pigments and apply the gesso to the wood). Should a light or white finish be required, all knots in the wood must be covered with shellac, else they will appear (bleed) through the paint.

Having praised the superior qualities of acrylic gesso for most purposes described in this manual, I must add that this material lacks the flowing quality of traditional gesso prepared from gilders' clay. This ancient material (described in Chapter 3) follows perfectly the conformation of the most intricate carvings, enveloping them smoothly and never registering brush marks. This is not the case with acrylic gesso.

Marbling

Wood painted in a manner that imitates marble surfaces appeared in Italy during the age of the Baroque at the end of the 16th century, and elsewhere in Europe a few decades later. After the Rococo style that ended with the French Revolution, the technique lost its currency. Whether economy originally dictated its use is doubtful; this manner of decor was favored by affluent patrons and, in fact, became more fashionable than the use of authentic marble. But imitation in paint was not confined to representations of marble surfaces alone. All kinds of wood grain were also simulated, chiefly by means of flexible combs. This technique was in common usage until the beginning of this century. But, all historic considerations aside, the art of marbling offers an endless source of delightful manipulations. Its applications can be many: decoration of cabinets, table tops, chairs, lamps, shelves, pedestals for antique objects, consoles, etc.

Marbling can be executed with two distinctive techniques: glazing or scumbling. The colors, as well as the gesso used for this purpose, will be of the *acrylic* kind only; the properties of these materials allow us to greatly simplify the involved procedures. Because the paint becomes water-insoluble when dry, layers can be superimposed at will. Moreover, the capacity of these paints to completely hide the underlying colors (when used with little dilution), or to allow repeated glazing when greatly diluted, makes them ideally suited to our tasks.

The glazing technique is by far the simplest one, relying on two principal operations: opaque underpainting and transparent overpainting. The underpainting is our acrylic gesso foundation. It must be applied very smoothly, showing no brush marks, and must be completely dry before the glaze is applied. As to the color of the gesso, the sky is the limit. But no matter which color you choose, the underlying

FIGURE 14. *Left to right: scriptliner, large soft hair brush, flat sable brush, round soft hair brush.*

FIGURE 15. *Left to right: utility brush, fan brush, stipple brush, flat soft hair brush.*

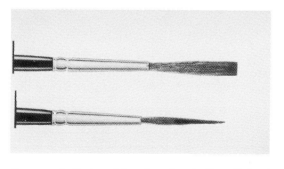

FIGURE 16. *Striper (above) and scriptliner (below).*

color must be lighter than the glaze on top of it. Remember, when I refer to a glaze, the term indicates a sufficient degree of transparency to allow the underlying color to prevail, more or less, depending on the effect you desire.

The marble effect seen in Color Plate 1 was carried out in the following manner. The raw wood surface was painted with several layers of white acrylic gesso to cover up its grain and to produce (after sand-papering) a perfectly smooth surface. Next, red acrylic paint was applied smoothly to the dry gesso foundation, without showing any brush marks. When this dried, thin black acrylic paint was brushed on, and while the paint was still wet, a piece of damp sponge was pressed against it in an irregular fashion, lifting off the black paint more or less, thus revealing the red ground underneath and producing varie-gated patterns. When dry, the surface was waxed.

In Fig. 12, the object was covered, again very smoothly, with light gray gesso (white acrylic gesso mixed with a little black acrylic paint). Next, a thin black wash was spread over the entire surface and lifted in spots, while still wet, with a paper towel. This operation allowed the gray color within to reappear in intriguing patterns.

In Color Plate 2, the ground was light yellow (white acrylic gesso, ochre, and some cadmium yellow) and the overpainting was done with burnt umber. Here a piece of wet sponge was instrumental (while the umber was wet) in producing an effect such as seen in the texture of some woods. When you use a sponge, its particular nature should be considered, because differ-ent patterns will result from the use of natural or synthetic sponges. Also the man-ner in which the sponge is pressed into the paint accounts for a particular effect. The same applies to the texture and absorbent qualities of paper towels and tissues.

An identical technique was applied in Fig. 13. Here the ground was also light gray; the glaze was mixed from phthalocyanine green and burnt siena, which neutralized the aggressive color of the green. Cheesecloth was used while the glaze was wet to uncover the gray color within. In one place, a brush lifted the darker overpaint, thus suggesting a vein in the structure of the marble.

Of course there are many more variations left open, challenging the inventive capacity of the craftsman.

Now we shall proceed to describe the second method, that of scumbling. The word scumble means that light paint was used on top of a darker foundation. This light paint will be mixed with white in order to show up on the darker underpainting. Once white enters into the mixture, the paint loses its transparent quality. Because of the more complex technique involved, brushes are our principal tools. These should possess various special characteristics, for the imprint of a particular tool will account for the effect achieved. Thus, a scriptliner, striper, round and flat sable brushes (Figs. 14, 15, and 16) will find their uses in addition to any conceivable tool you might dream up to produce those fantastic configurations seen in marble veneers.

In Color Plate 3, opaque marbling was done on a dark gray ground in lighter and darker bluish-green. The scumbling on the central panel, framed in a gilded molding, received a larger admixture of white.

The example in Color Plate 4 is much smaller; the very light areas, made of

FIGURE 17. *Wet green-gray acrylic paint foundation was marbled with white acrylic gesso, using sable brushes.*

FIGURE 18. *Background panel was painted greenish-gray (ultramarine, ochre, acrylic gesso); simulated marbling was executed on wet paint with white acrylic gesso and scriptliner. Collection of the author.*

wood, but simulating marble, were painted with white acrylic gesso, stained with a little ultramarine and umber. The rectangular "marble" veneers combine both opaque and glazing techniques; hence, in this particular instance, the foundation was a light color. In contrast to the pure glazing procedure, "accidental" effects and those produced by mechanical means are fairly absent. The marbling was carried out with one round sable brush, using a very liquid burnt umber paint spread over a white ground.

Color Plates 5 and 6 represent the capital and plinth of a neo-classic column from about 1800, acquired in a very poor state of preservation. On the base (Color Plate 6) the marbling was done with a mixture of umber and phthalocyanine blue (hence it appears almost black) into which, while still wet, white gesso was scumbled with the scriptliner. The sleeve at the base of the capital (Color Plate 5) carries pink with effects of white graining. The acanthus leaves (Color Plate 5) were recovered with silver leaf (see Chapter 3) and then glazed with viridian green oil color. The remaining woodwork was gilded and antiqued (see Chapter 3). Thus the capital shows a color scheme of pink, silvery green, and gold.

The same technique as used on the plinth was employed in painting the top of the console and the background panel for the sculptured relief in Figs. 17 and 18. This is the simplest method of marbling —and a very satisfactory one: on a wet, greenish-gray, opaque surface of a more or less unvaried acrylic color, the marble effect was made with a scriptliner and striper in a free swinging manner, using the white gesso as the only over-painting color.

2
FINISHING NON-ANTIQUES

Those interested in the craft of making debilitated antiques presentable are less likely to face "objects of virtu"—in the language of the trade, art objects and curios of value—than non-antiques or, at best, semi-antiques, of small initial value, but great potential for pleasure or even profit. But even here, distinction must be made between objects possessing merit and those which must be considered hopeless. By hopeless, I mean utilitarian objects of poor design, where the re-creation of their original condition would be pointless.

Cleaning and repairing veneers

I should, of course, remind the reader that the word "condition" refers to the surface finish alone, not to repairs that require expert knowledge of carpentry; repairs involving woodwork or veneer should be entrusted to a skilled cabinet maker before attempting the restoration of the finish.

The finishes we are apt to encounter on non-antiques are basically those commonly found on veneers and raw wood: varnish, lacquer, paint, etc.

Refinishing veneers usually means partially or totally removing the old polish, and repairing cracks and scratches (see Chapter 1). Partial removal of the polish suggests that surface defects are minor, amounting chiefly to abrasions and shallow scratches which do not involve the wood to any marked extent. These can be eliminated in most instances by rubbing them with a paste prepared from pumicestone and linseed or crude oil; or a much milder abrasive made of rottenstone and oil. I suggest using a piece of felt for rubbing.

The polish can be completely removed in one of two ways: by using paint remover, or by sandpapering. Commerical paint remover comes in liquid or gel form.

The latter is most useful when applied to a vertical surface, where the gel remains without dripping off. After the old varnish softens, it can be scraped off easily with a spatula or an ordinary putty knife. This done, the surface should be well cleaned with painters' thinner or turpentine to eliminate the residue of paraffin that all paint removers contain. When left on the surface, such residue would impair the subsequent revarnishing or repolishing of the veneer.

Re-surfacing raw wood

If the object carries debris of old paints, varnishes, or lacquers, in addition to various surface damages, what will our procedure be? If the basic design is in reasonably good taste, giving it a proper finish will undoubtedly turn the ugly duckling into a thing of beauty.

First, paint remover will be called into action, and then, more likely than not, sandpapering with carborundum paper. (The appropriate coarseness of the paper will depend on the nature of the surface.) A finer flint paper can be used next. Repairs of cracks, holes, gouges, etc., should be done at this stage (see Chapter 1). After the surface is rendered reasonably smooth —one need not necessarily go overboard in this direction since a slightly irregular finish has its charms—the subsequent operations should be carried out as follows on the clean, raw wood that is now exposed.

The surface can be painted a solid color, using any commercial interior paint that dries flat and leaves no brushmarks, then glazed as in Chapter 1. For effects like Figs. 19-22 four basic colors can be used as the solid undercoat: white, red, yellow, and blue. These can be intermixed to render hues such as pink (white and red), green (yellow and blue), or purple (red and

blue), and all can be lightened with white. Our choice of these basic colors is limited inasmuch as they must be light enough to allow the superimposed glaze to register effectively. Of course, certain parts of an object can be painted in opaque colors: for example, the top of a table may be glazed, given an over-all light effect, but its legs could be of any solid, dark color.

Now our glaze will be produced from Rockhard Finish Varnish or spar varnish thinned with a little turpentine mixed with the following oil colors: black and umber; black, umber, and Venetian red; umber and Venetian red; or any one of the dark Mars colors. It is important not to make the paint too dense, else it will lack the requisite transparency. Except in the spatter technique (Fig. 19), the glaze is always applied to the entire surface to be treated, left on it for a few minutes to allow the film to set to some extent, then textured with various tools. The greater the viscosity, the more precise will be the execution of the pattern; a very limpid paint film will not properly hold the imprint of the various implements used to produce the patterns.

In Figs. 19-22, just one glaze of black and burnt umber was used.

In Fig. 19, on the left side of the panel, the glaze was spread solidly and then stippled, holding the narrow brush in Fig. 23 vertically to the surface and tapping. The spatter on the right side was produced by flipping the same brush, dipped into the glazing medium. The less liquid the brush holds, the finer the spray will appear. A *very* fine spray can be obtained by rubbing a brush (a toothbrush is best) against a closely woven wire screen held over the wooden surface.

In Fig. 20, the underpainting was yellow ochre and the pattern, in part suggesting

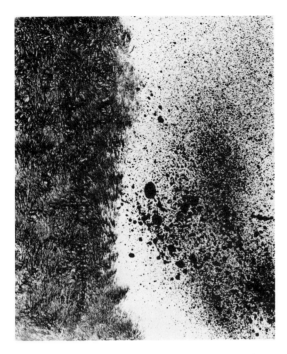

FIGURE 19. *On dry white ground (flat white interior paint), glaze of Rockhard Finish Varnish and some turpentine, mixed with ivory black, Venetian red oil color was stippled with brush (left) and spattered with same brush (right).*

FIGURE 20. *Glaze of ivory black, Venetian red thinned with Rockhard Finish Varnish, was applied to foundation of ochre flat interior paint, textured with rubber combs.*

FIGURE 21. *Red flat interior paint was textured with brush (top and bottom), cheesecloth (middle), using the same glaze in this illustration as that used in Fig. 20.*

FIGURE 22. *Blue flat interior paint was textured with same glaze as Fig. 20, using comb (left), cheesecloth (middle), newspaper pressed and lifted (right).*

31

FIGURE 23. *Left to right: flat bristle brush, stiff brush for stippling, rubber comb (top right), metal comb (bottom right).*

wood grain, was executed with the combs in Fig. 23.

Fig. 21 shows the marks of the broad brush in Fig. 23, except for the light stripe where cheesecloth was pressed into the wet glaze. This was all done on a red ground.

Fig. 22 has a blue ground. The narrow metal comb in Fig. 23 was used on the left side of the panel, cheesecloth in the middle, and the curious pattern on the right side is the result of newsprint pressed into the wet paint surface and then lifted.

Color Plate 7 shows the effects of just one glaze—asphaltum dissolved in turpentine—applied to different underpaintings with a resulting variety of effects. The four grounds are white; white mixed with ochre; ochre; and cadmium yellow.

The examples introduced here are basic to the technique; they can, of course, be expanded to suit individual preferences. Different tools can be brought into action; underpaintings and glazes of different colors can be employed; and so can metallic applications (see Chapter 3).

Reconditioning a rustic cabinet

Now I shall demonstrate the reconditioning of some utilitarian objects that could not, by any stretch of the imagination, be considered "antiques." All of these were treated according to the simple method I have discussed.

When retrieved from a children's play room, the rustic cabinet in Figs. 24 and 25 was literally a wreck, with nearly all its original finish gone. (Unfortunately, no photo of its original condition is available.) My first concern was to fill its nicks and holes with wood putty; for very shallow cracks modeling paste was used; and all this was well sanded. The repaired surface first received a smooth priming of a dull wood color: a mixture of ochre, umber and

COLOR PLATE 1. *White acrylic gesso was followed by red acrylic underpainting, glazed with black acrylic. Pattern was produced with sponge.*

COLOR PLATE 2. *Yellow acrylic gesso foundation was glazed with burnt umber acrylic color, then patterned with wet sponge.*

COLOR PLATE 3. *Dark gray acrylic gesso was mixed with lighter and darker bluish-green color, applied with round sable brushes and sponge. Central panel (within gilded molding) received light gray underpainting. Here same colors were applied in glazes (without white).*

COLOR PLATE 4. *Light areas, simulating marble, were painted with white acrylic gesso, tinted lightly with ultramarine and umber acrylic paint. Simulated marble veneers are burnt umber acrylic glaze over white acrylic gesso. Flat and round sable brushes were used.*

COLOR PLATE 5. *Acanthus leaves were covered with silver leaf, glazed with viridian green oil color. Scrolls were gilded, antiqued. Neck was veined with pink and white acrylic color.*

COLOR PLATE 6. *Plinth was covered opaquely with phthalocyanine blue and umber, followed by white marbling painted with scriptliner into wet underpainting. Sleeve received phthalocyanine green mixed with burnt siena, followed by white marbling scumbled into wet paint (all acrylic). Gold parts were goldleafed, antiqued.*

COLOR PLATE 7. *Luminous effects were produced with asphaltum, dissolved in turpentine, glazed in various densities over (left to right) white, white and ochre, ochre, cadmium yellow.*

COLOR PLATE 8. *Drawers were underpainted in flat white interior paint, side compartments in yellow; then drawers were glazed with Rockhard Finish Varnish, Mars brown oil color, textured with turpentine moistened sponge. Yellow side panels were glazed with Rockhard Finish Varnish, black, Venetian red, textured with rubber combs.*

Color Plate 9. *Surrounded by masking tape, star was sprayed with gold paint (from aerosol can), antiqued with burnt umber acrylic color; rest of top surface was marbled like drawers in Color Plate 8, but texture was produced with paper towel. All borders and legs were painted with gray-green flat interior paint, then varnished with Rockhard Finish Varnish.*

Color Plate 10. *Lamp bases, cut from old table legs, were heavily covered with traditional gesso (glue size and whiting), then re-gessoed with dark color (phthalocyanine blue, Venetian red, whiting, glue size). Shaft at left was sprayed with gold paint, shaft at right with silver paint (from aerosol cans). Gold was antiqued with orange shellac, silver glazed with viridian green oil color mixed with Rockhard Finish Varnish. Gold received gray, silver received red patina prepared from acrylic paint. Bases of both were marbled.*

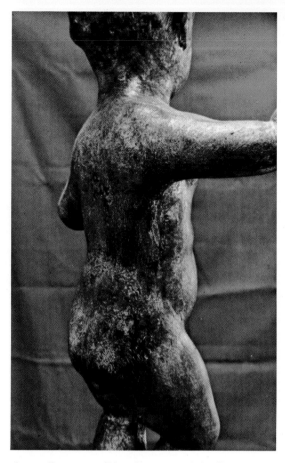

COLOR PLATE 11. *Base and section to right of ornaments are restorations, gilded and antiqued to match 18th century finish of original piece.*

COLOR PLATE 12. *Figurine was originally unappealing flesh color. Refinished by covering with silver leaf, it was then antiqued.*

COLOR PLATE 13. *Plinth was surfaced with black acrylic paint, silvered, lightly sandpapered, coated with orange shellac, given dusty patina to attain an antique look.*

COLOR PLATE 14. *Terracotta head broken at the line of the neck, was repaired with Liquitex acrylic modeling paste, coated with acrylic gesso colored with red iron oxide and ochre dry pigments.*

COLOR PLATE 15. *Bronze and copper fragments show various colors, surface incrustations produced by corrosive chemicals.*

COLOR PLATE 16. *Object at left was buried in soil saturated with copper sulphate and water (1:3). Dug up after three weeks, it was re-buried for three more weeks in soil saturated with acetic acid and salt. Center object was wrapped in cloth saturated with iron chloride, sparsely sprinkled with ammonium chloride, kept in cloth for about 10 hours. Object at right was treated with Incra Patine and hydrochloric acid as described in Chapter 6.*

white. When this dried, the graining was painted with a slightly darker version of the same color mixture (plus burnt siena) in a semi-opaque manner, that is, diluted somewhat with water. Only acrylic paints were used.

The simulated wood grain (Fig. 25) was produced with only one brush, an old soft hair blender, half its length stiffened by dried paint.

There was no problem in painting the plain dark color or the thin single stripe. Although this is usually done freehand by specialists, I resorted to the use of masking tape.

Reconditioning stools

The next objects are the four lowly stools in Figs. 26-29. Their original indifferent color was first overpainted with light blue-green flat interior paint.

The seat of the stool in Fig. 26 was glazed with Rockhard Finish Varnish mixed with Mars brown dry pigment (any good resin varnish could have been used for this purpose). The marbling was achieved by pressing a sponge moistened with turpentine into the wet glaze.

In Fig. 27, the process was more complex. Here the seat was painted with flat white, interior paint, then glazed as in Fig. 26. Next white, ochre, phthalocyanine blue, and phthalocyanine green dry pigments—each mixed separately with turpentine to watercolor consistency—were spattered into the wet glaze. A stiff bristle brush was used for this purpose, and an extra thin scriptliner was used to draw the linear structure of the marble conglomerate.

The seat of the stool in Fig. 28 was silvered, and that in Fig. 29 was gilded; both the silver and gold were sprayed from aerosol cans. The sprayed surfaces were then protected with Rockhard Finish

FIGURE 24. *Repaired condition of once ruined finish of a rustic cabinet. Deep nicks and holes were filled with wood putty; shallow cracks were filled with acrylic modeling paste.*

FIGURE 25. *Top surface was then primed to approximate dull wood color (acrylic gesso mixed with ochre, umber dry pigments) over which grain was painted with darker version of same mixture (plus burnt siena) diluted with water to semi-opaque consistency.*

 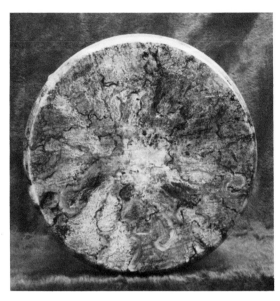

FIGURE 26. *Bluish-green flat interior paint was first used to obliterate original unattractive finish of all four stools in Figs. 26–29. In this example, top was glazed with Rockhard Finish Varnish mixed with Mars brown pigment. Texture was produced by pressing turpentine moistened sponge into wet glaze. Same varnish was used for final finish of this and Figs. 27–29.*

FIGURE 27. *Seat was painted with flat white interior paint, then glazed (always on dry surface) as in Fig. 26. Next, white, ochre, phthalocyanine blue and green dry pigments were mixed separately with turpentine to a thin consistency and spattered into wet glaze. Faint marks of marble conglomerate effects were done with scriptliner.*

FIGURE 28. *Surface was first sprayed with silver paint (from aerosol can), isolated with Rockhard Finish Varnish, then glazed heavily with same varnish (as in Figs. 26 and 27) and finally textured with ball of crumpled newsprint.*

FIGURE 29. *Surface was sprayed with gold paint from aerosol can, isolated with varnish, glazed and textured as in Fig. 28.*

Varnish, and the same varnish, thinned a little with turpentine, was used for the glaze on the dry surface. The pattern on both surfaces was achieved by pressing and twisting a ball of crumpled newsprint into the wet glaze, prepared with Mars brown.

Finally, the seats of all four stools were varnished and the legs antiqued with greenish-brown oil color.

Reconditioning a sewing table

The sewing table (seen in its original condition in Fig. 30) was first stripped of its old finish with paint remover, then sandpapered. The step by step process of refinishing developed as follows (Fig. 31):

Step 1: The top was underpainted in flat white interior paint.

Step 2: The drawers were also underpainted in flat white interior paint and the side compartments in yellow.

Step 3: A circular template, cut out of paper, was attached with rubber cement to the middle of the top surface. Marbling was produced around the template and across the entire top by pressing absorbent paper into a glaze made of Rockhard Finish Varnish thinned with turpentine and mixed with Mars brown. The same treatment was accorded to the drawers, but here a turpentine moistened sponge was used for achieving a marble effect.

Step 4: Maskoid was painted around the template. (This is a liquid frisket which dries to a paint-proof masking film; after painting, it can be peeled off like a film of rubber.) The template was removed, the circular shape painted black, and the Maskoid around the circle was rubbed or peeled off, thus leaving a perfect black circle.

Step 5: The star was drawn on the black

FIGURE 30. *Ruined sewing table (seen here in original damaged condition) was stripped of old finish with paint remover and sandpapered, preparatory to steps in Fig. 31. For result of transformation, see Color Plates 8 and 9.*

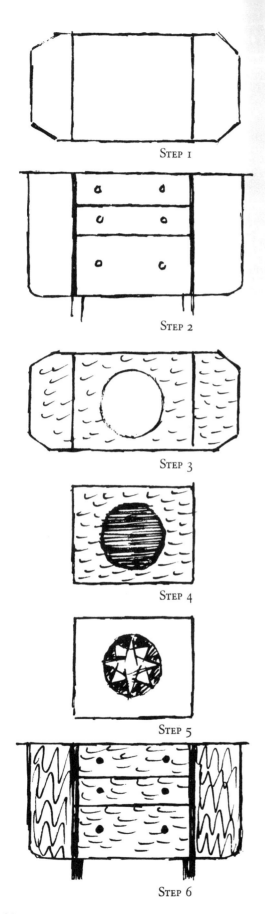

STEP 1

STEP 2

STEP 3

STEP 4

STEP 5

STEP 6

ground with a light colored pencil and the edges of the star were surrounded by masking tape. The rest of the table top was also covered, whereupon the star was sprayed with gold paint from an aerosol can. The star was then antiqued with burnt umber acrylic paint and the tape and other covering removed.

Step 6: The yellow side compartments were glazed with a mixture of Rockhard Finish Varnish, black, and Venetian red, and patterned with all three sides of a rubber comb (Fig. 23). Last, the legs and all the borders were painted with dark gray flat interior paint; the straight lines of these borders were made with the aid of masking tape. The entire piece (Color Plates 8 and 9) was then protected with Rockhard Finish Varnish, giving it a high gloss. If a matte finish is desired, Behloid Satin Dull Table Top, Semigloss Eggshell Finish, Dead Flat Finish, or similar products will provide it. However, these do not possess the imperviousness of the Rockhard Varnish which, incidentally, can be deprived of its high gloss by polishing it with a paste of pumice powder and oil (linseed or crude oil).

FIGURE 31. *Step 1: Top underpainted in flat white interior paint. Step 2: Drawers underpainted in flat white interior paint, side compartments in yellow. Step 3: Round paper template attached with rubber cement; top and drawers marbled with Rockhard Finish Varnish, Mars brown. Step 4: Maskoid painted around template; template removed; circular shape painted black; Maskoid peeled off. Step 5: Star drawn with light colored pencil, surrounded with masking tape, sprayed gold from aerosol can, antiqued with burnt umber acrylic; tape removed. Step 6: Side compartments glazed with Rockhard Finish Varnish mixed with black, Venetian red, then patterned with rubber comb; legs, borders painted with dark gray flat interior paint, aided by masking tape; entire piece coated with Rockhard Finish Varnish.*

From table legs to table lamps

The attractive table lamps in Color Plate 10 were made from sections of legs (Fig. 32) which once supported a dining room table top. The legs were found in a country antique shop, already deprived of their one-time finish. The metamorphosis of the legs to lamps developed step by step as follows:

Step 1: An electrician drilled through the shafts to provide entry for the wiring.

Step 2: The rather rough surfaces had to be heavily gessoed. Here the traditional gesso (size and whiting) was used, and well sandpapered. (This operation would have been quite difficult if acrylic gesso were used.)

Step 3: The plan was to gild one, and to silver the other ribbed shaft, and then to marble the tops and bases. Hence both columns were gessoed again from top to bottom in a dark color: phthalocyanine blue and Venetian red mixed with gesso (to make the phthalocyanine color disperse in the glue size, the pigment had to be wetted first with methyl alcohol). Steel wool was used to smooth the second gesso coat, whereupon the surfaces were made non-absorbent by coating them with acrylic polymer medium.

Step 4: The tops and bases to be marbled were protected by masking them with paper, and the shafts were sprayed with metallic gold and silver from aerosol cans (Krylon gold and silver spray).

Step 5: Upon drying, the gold was antiqued with orange shellac, and the silver was glazed with viridian green oil color thinned with Rockhard Finish Varnish.

Step 6: Then followed the patination. The gilded shaft was covered entirely with

FIGURE 32. *Sections of old table legs were transformed into "antique" lamp bases with gesso, gold, silver sprays and patinas. See Color Plate 10 for finished product.*

45

a gray patina (thinned acrylic gesso and umber) and the silvered shaft with red patina (acrylic paint). While still wet, the patina was removed with a moist cloth from all the prominent ribs, allowing the gray or red substance to remain only in the recessions.

Step 7: Last, marbling was done on the tops and bases. A glaze of phthalocyanine green and burnt siena, dispersed in acrylic polymer medium, followed, giving intriguing color variations to the whole. Into this wet glaze, white marbling effects were painted, in one case, with white acrylic color (white gesso) using a scriptliner and striper; in the second case, with a white and ochre scumble, treated with a wet sponge. On non-antiques, we may use industrial gold and silver spray paints. I deviated here from the traditional manner of gold and silver leafing simply to give the reader an easy method to use on such objects—a method that I would *not* employ on bona fide antiques or objects of value.

A note about industrial products

In any consideration of wood finishes, the products of H. Behlen & Bro., preeminent in the field, must be mentioned. I shall describe a few materials from their very extensive list and mention the uses to which they lend themselves.

Alcohol soluble (aniline) dyes can be added to white or orange shellac to influence their color.

Color Dissolvent, Decolorant, and *Bleach Booster* are the most effective bleaching agents for wood; I have even used them on textiles when all available cleaning agents were ineffective. Here is the recommended procedure. Apply one coat of Color Dissolvent and be sure to wet evenly; do not saturate. Within a few minutes, apply a generous coat of Decolorant and allow four hours' drying time. Do *not* use more than one coat of Color Dissolvent. For greater color bleaching, apply a second coat of Decolorant and again allow four hours' drying time for complete bleaching. If water marks or residual chemical stains are still present, use a final liberal coat of Bleach Booster. The solutions cannot be intermixed.

Rockhard Finish Varnish has been thoroughly discussed in this chapter.

Burn-in sticks: In the sections on repairing wood surfaces, I have described procedures that can be carried out without much difficulty by the amateur wood craftsman. Professionals, however, use a process commonly known as burning-in. I refer to it here for the benefit of those who may wish to acquire professional skill, for this work —when properly done—assuredly entails some difficulties. The materials used for this operation are known as burn-in sticks. These are made from shellac mixed with other resins, and they come in a great variety of colors to match every known kind of wood. Two kinds of burn-in sticks are available. One category is used for lacquer finishes, the other for shellac and varnish finishes.

In addition, special equipment is necessary to perform the task. A source of heat is needed to melt the stick, so that it can be applied to the damaged areas. The safest heater is the electric knife heater which produces clean, constant heat. An alcohol lamp or a Bunsen burner (Fig. 7) can also be used for this purpose. The knife (not unlike our palette knives in Fig. 4) must be sufficiently heated to melt the stick without scorching it. These knives are used in pairs to avoid delay, heating one while the other is being used.

To repair bruises, dents, deep scratches, or gouges, the surrounding surface must be free of wax and dirt and relatively smooth. Only enough material to fill the damaged area is melted on the knife; when liquefied, the material is placed on the far edge of the damaged area and pulled into the scratch, depression, or scar.

Once the hole is filled, care must be taken to smooth the surface and make it level with the rest of the work. This can be accomplished in several ways, such as scraping the surplus with a sharp knife or sandpapering. One of the best methods of leveling the burned-in area is to use a non-abrasive liquid, such as Abrasol, with a felt pad. This liquid levels the area fast and leaves no oily residue.

Qualarenue is a product especially formulated for renovating old, cracked, checked, or alligatored finishes. Qualarenue No. 1 amalgamates or blends the old finish, and Qualarenue No. 2 finishes the job of renovation. At times, the addition of Qualatone Solvent 710 is required to quicken the amalgamation process. Instructions for applying these products are noted on the labels of the bottles.

Lacquers

Since we have touched on the methods of industrial technology, a brief reference should be made to modern lacquer products.

It must be understood that lacquers are distinctly different from water based acrylics, oils, or varnishes. In fact, when used on top of any finish produced with these three materials, lacquers may prove to be a powerful solvent, softening the underlying layers. Hence, as a general rule, lacquer coating should be applied to raw wood (treated first with a lacquer based sealer), then sprayed with clear lacquer or lacquer colors. I say "sprayed" because these products, known as alkyd enamel finishes, come in aerosol cans.

Consider, for example, a possible lacquer finish on the table lamps in Color Plate 10. The first coat could be a solid lacquer film, gradually built up to appreciable thickness to cover up surface imperfections in the wood. After sandpapering, one or more colored sprays could be used interchangeably and lightly, then sandpapered or treated with steel wool. As a final coat, marbling or patination could be carried out in any desirable material—oil or acrylic colors.

What advantages does such treatment offer? First, speed and instant drying. Second, smoothness that no brush, no matter how skillfully used, could produce. In finishing real antiques, of course, such methods must be avoided—anything that suggests mechanical or industrial processes would be inappropriate. However, when dealing with non-antiques, one may well avail himself of industrial techniques if these appear to be advantageous.

3
GILDING
AND
SILVERING

It bears repeating that all of the techniques described here are designed to be mastered by the layman—anticipating results comparable to those attained by the expert.

Gold leafing

This most noble of all the gilding processes provides magnificent effects, as we all know.

The professional gilder uses standard gold leaf which comes in sheets 3⅜" square, and requires very sensitive handling. The leaf is taken up from the tissue paper backing with a sharp, straight bladed knife and placed on the so-called gilder's cushion (Fig. 33) of chamois leather. The leaf is then cut carefully (so as not to injure the chamois), picked up with the gilder's tip (Fig. 33), and attached to the assigned spaces as I will describe presently. It is necessary to rub the tip lightly against one's hair before picking up the leaf; this ritual generates an electric impulse that will cause the metal to adhere to the tip.

However, by using the material known as Swift Patent Gold Leaf, you can eliminate the main difficulty in handling the fragile gold. The leaf, which is *attached* to the underlying tissue paper, can be handled with one's hand; it can be cut with scissors to any desired size and put *with* the adhering tissue paper on the assigned place. Two qualities of gold are available: 23 karat "deep gold leaf" and the 16½ karat "pale gold leaf." We shall use the first because its color has a more antique character.

Gold leafing step by step

The step by step process is as follows:

Step 1: The surface to be gilded should be primed with either white gilders' clay or Heins red, yellow, or blue burnishing clay. White clay comes in powder form, which should be well dispersed in a warm size prepared in a double boiler from ¾ oz. rabbit skin glue and 1 pt. water; the resulting gesso should be smooth and have the consistency of heavy cream. Heins clays come in soft paste form; warm up as much of the paste as you need for the work at hand, and mix it with the size to a brushable consistency.

The material should be kept warm in the double boiler (not hot, which produces rapid dehydration). Apply it smoothly to the work surface with a soft hair brush, and allow this priming to dry well. As a rule, several primings will be required.

As to choice of color, gold leaf should be applied to red or yellow priming; silver looks best on blue. Of course, white can be used for either one of these metals. As a matter of fact, antique gildings always carry a substantial white ground under the red or yellow one.

Step 2: The resulting surface should be well polished, first with extra fine sandpaper, and finally with fine steel wool or garnet paper.

Step 3: The method of attaching gold leaf suggested here is my own; after much experience with all kinds of processes, I consider it the most agreeable to use, especially for the amateur.

First, glue size is made in a double boiler and allowed to cool. This size is weaker than the one used for gesso; the formula is ½ oz. rabbit skin glue and 1 pt. water. At normal room temperature, it will turn to a gel. The soft, gelled substance should then be reduced to mush with a spatula, then rubbed with one's fingers or with a bristle brush onto the primed (gessoed) surface.

Now, suppose we intend to gild a strip, perhaps 2″ wide and 8″ long. This is as large a surface as we would treat with the adhesive at one time. We coat the entire strip with gel. By the time we have worked the gel into the last inch of the strip, the first few inches may have attained the right condition of tackiness: the surface is neither too wet nor too dry. (If too wet, the gold leaf will tear; if too dry, it will not adhere.) If the priming is quite absorbent, it will require two separate sizings with the gel before applying the leaf.

Step 4: Place the leaf face down on the tacky priming. Gently press the tissue paper into the surface and then lift the tissue, leaving the gold leaf stuck in the assigned position. This method is referred to as water gilding.

It should be mentioned that one can attach gold leaf with practically any conceivable adhesive, such as gold (Japan) size, acrylic medium or gel, shellac, or gamboge (see Chapter 8) which is especially adaptable for this purpose. Leaf can also be placed on a slightly tacky gesso ground, to which it will adhere firmly. But when burnishing is planned, water gilding and the use of an elastic priming (such as a clay ground) are best.

FIGURE 33. *Gilder's cushion and tip. Homemade cushion is wood panel (5″ x 7″) covered with sturdy chamois leather, stuffed with cotton. Gilder's tip is 4″ wide, made of squirrel hair set in cardboard.*

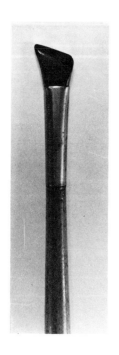

FIGURE 34. (*Left*) *Agate burnisher.* FIGURE 35. (*Right*) *Two dental tools, steel burnisher, wood stylus, modeling tool, scraper.*

Burnishing and antiquing

If you wish, a second gold application (using the same means of attachment) may follow. This will impart a more solid appearance to the gilded surface, but not a greater sheen.

To produce a high gloss, the surface will require burnishing. The best instrument for this purpose is one made of agate (Fig. 34); a steel burnisher (Fig. 35), such as used for polishing copper plates in etching, is also serviceable. Gentle but firm rubbing of the surface will produce the desired high gloss. If its original color is to be retained, the gilding can now receive a protective layer of white shellac. An "antique" appearance can be obtained by coating it with orange shellac and/or gamboge (dissolved in hot turpentine); finally, a solution of asphaltum in turpentine will further deepen the color of the gold. The first will impart a warm, orangey tone; the second will provide a brilliant warm yellow glow; and the third will darken the color to a warm brown.

Other patinas can be obtained by mixing alcohol soluble dyes with white or orange shellac. Even acrylic paint will serve well for this purpose.

Moreover, dragon's blood can also be used for antiquing. This is a dark red resinous exudate of the rattan palm that grows in eastern Asia. Contrary to reports in some manuals, I have found that it dissolves readily in cold turpentine. Like gamboge, it can also be cooked in linseed oil and applied as an oil glaze. However, in this form it is a very slow drier, especially when painted over nonabsorbent surfaces. Therefore, to accelerate its drying, it should receive an addition of cobalt dryer in the amount of a few drops of dryer to a teaspoonful of dragon's blood. It must be understood that such a resin-oil-dryer application will darken in time, thus adding to the semblance of age—a circumstance that may be welcome when the appearance of great antiquity is desirable.

To repeat: the gilding can be glazed with

orange shellac, gamboge, dragon's blood, acrylic paint, asphaltum, or a succession of *all* these liquids. Should one wish to produce a rather dark finish, using the true gold leaf is extravagant—metal leaf will do very well.

Artificial aging

How does one produce the worn, damaged, mottled appearance of an old gilt surface? This can be attained by careful and judicious sandpapering of the surface to remove some of its gilding; steel wool or a scraper (Fig. 35) can also be used for this purpose. Or you can brush raw or burnt umber acrylic paint over the entire surface and daub it with a wad of cheesecloth; this wiping will remove much of the paint and produce a glazed, mottled appearance such as we often see on gilded surfaces that are centuries old.

To increase the severity of the effect, try *both* sandpapering (or scraping) and glazing with umber (some black can be added to reduce the brown coloring). Remember that acrylic colors dry rapidly and should be treated with cheesecloth immediately after they are brushed on. If overdone, acrylic paint can be easily removed with acetone or lacquer thinner. Preferably, all this should be done on a red clay priming; however, yellow and white priming can also be used for achieving certain effects.

Where all these manipulations do not quite match the appearance of a centuries old, darkened (but otherwise undamaged) gilded surface, here is another method. After initial applications of orange shellac, the surface should be treated with wax-resin compound (see Chapter 8) mixed with some burnt or raw umber pigment. If needed, black pigment may also be added to the mixture.

Finally, one operation will add still more to the appearance of old age: rubbing some rottenstone into the dry surface. The gray powder will settle in the crevices and cling tenaciously to every crack, no matter how minute.

Now the question may arise, have we perpetrated an act of deception in artificially producing the appearance of age? Hardly. A deception can be only looked upon as such when the intention is kept a secret—and when the effect is not good enough to appear "genuine." We should remember that in ancient paintings and decor, tin coated with appropriate varnishes was often used to simulate gold. During the 17th and 18th centuries, "marble" surfaces were produced by means of paint; this was not considered a falsification, but rather a clever exercise in *trompe l'oeil* (fool the eye) art.

FIGURE 36. *Design in gold leaf on black ground, with outlines incised in graffito technique.*

Designs in gold and graffito technique

There remains one gold application which I have not yet discussed: the execution or restoration of designs. In Fig. 36, the design (which embellishes the flat surface of a picture frame) was carried out in gold leaf on a black ground, and its outlines were incised in a graffito technique. Graffito simply means scratching into a dry or wet layer of color. When doing this, the underlying layer of color must always be considered because when you incise the top color, the underlying color comes into view. In our case, the graffito lines are white because the underlying layer of paint (beneath the black) was white.

Now let us assume that part of the original design has been destroyed. How are we going to restore it?

Step 1: Since a decorative design always repeats itself, we shall trace (on a piece of translucent tracing paper) an existing pattern found elsewhere on the object, a section identical with that to be replaced.

Step 2: This done, white chalk should be rubbed into the reverse side of the tracing paper, which will allow us to trace the design onto the black surface in white outlines.

Step 3: Next the entire design should be accurately painted within its linear contours —painted with an adhesive that will hold the gold leaf. Our customary adhesive— glue size—would not be adaptable for this operation; therefore we shall use Japan gold size. When it solidifies to a point where only a slight tackiness remains, the gold leaf, with its adhering tissue paper, should be placed over the design and firmly pressed down with the tissue paper, which is then removed. In a few hours, when the adhesive dries completely, the gold leaf

that extends beyond the design (and has therefore failed to attach itself to the surface) should be wiped off with a soft hair brush.

Step 4: Lastly, the gold application may be antiqued and the graffito lines—if desired— can be incised. Because we are dealing here with a well solidified ground, a sharp instrument (such as the dental tools seen in Fig. 35) should be used for this purpose.

A different finish (originated in 17th century Spain) calls for a graffito treatment throughout (Fig. 37). We shall proceed here as follows:

Step 1: A gesso ground should be applied to the panel.

Step 2: Gold leaf should be attached to the entire area with any one of the adhesives mentioned (Japan size, acrylic medium or gel, shellac, and gamboge) and then protected with white shellac.

Step 3: When this dries, the design should be traced onto it. Now we can distinguish between the background and the design and use different colors for each. The paint used for this purpose is an emulsion prepared from the chosen oil color mixed with an equal quantity of a thick solution of gum Arabic (see Chapter 8): one part gum dissolved in one part hot water. Some umber oil paint should always be added to the mixture to accelerate drying and the whole should be well worked with a palette knife to produce a homogeneous substance. The design is then painted.

Step 4: Now the parallel graffito lines can be scratched into the wet, semi-dry, or almost dry paint. This can be done either with a sharpened pencil or a wooden stylus (Fig. 35). We use an emulsion for this purpose because no other paint is so well adapted for the graffito technique.

FIGURE 37. *Design in gold leaf. Overpainting in dark color; graffito lines appear golden (white in photo).*

In the example in Fig. 37, the ornament was gilded and then overpainted in a dark color, so the graffito marks reveal the gilded substratum. The background was painted a solid red and the frame around it in black. The area of the frame shows various graffito marks.

It should also be noted that the gilding does not appear as a solid surface in this graffito technique, but is seen as fine, detached lines. Thus, you may as well use an inexpensive metal leaf.

Applying metal leaf

To the inexperienced, metal leaf—imitation gold—appears to be more "golden" than the genuine stuff. The metal leaf is sturdier and comes in larger pieces (5½" square) than the true gold, but because the cheaper product is not attached to underlying tissue paper, its handling is more difficult. Moreover, its malleability cannot be compared to that of the true gold leaf; hence metal leaf does not react as well to burnishing. Is it therefore inferior? Far from it. This depends on the final effect we seek. Should

its surface become sufficiently obscured through antiquing, there is no reason why we should not use metal leaf, for in the end it will be indistinguishable from true gold leaf.

The application process does not differ from that of true gold leaf, except that it will be cut without the tissue paper and handled with one's fingers. To make this manipulation feasible, the scissors must be meticulously clean and free from any trace of grease; the fingers must be absolutely dry. In order to facilitate this, one should keep in readiness a bottle of alcohol and a dish of chalk, which will serve to clean the scissors as well as one's fingers.

Applying silver and aluminum leaf

Applying silver leaf is not easy because this material is exceedingly flimsy; although it comes with tissue paper, the leaf and underlying tissue paper are not attached. Nevertheless, we shall have to cut it (with its tissue paper) to the required size, and flip it off to the areas to be repaired, or use the professional gilder's tip and cushion (Fig. 33). The leaf can be attached with the same adhesives as gold or metal leaf.

Silver leaf is malleable; that is, it can be burnished and also antiqued in one of two ways. You can treat it with a greatly diluted solution of liver of sulphur (see Chapter 7); the indicated amount of water should be increased. If you plan to treat the silver with liver of sulphur, the leaf should not be attached with a water-based adhesive because when wetted, the leaf will most likely come off. Therefore, either Japan gold size or shellac should be used for the attachment. The liver of sulphur solution should be applied with a soft brush; as soon as the silver leaf begins to tarnish, the chemical should be washed off.

A simpler, quite effective method is to

tarnish the silver with glazes of black and umber acrylic paint. This can be done best with cheesecloth after first covering the silver with a protective coat of white shellac. It must be said, however, that unprotected silver leaf tarnishes in a relatively short time when exposed to air.

Just as in the case of imitation gold, imitation silver (which is made of aluminum) looks more genuine than true silver and is also considerably more substantial, hence much easier to handle. However, aluminum leaf will not tarnish as well when treated with acid. Therefore, in cases where a natural tarnish appears desirable, this material will not serve its purpose. Oddly enough, it will be most useful in simulating the effects of gold: we can produce a golden effect on aluminum leaf by coating it with one or several layers of orange shellac and, of course, other ingredients— such as brown and black acrylic paint glazes, gamboge, asphaltum, and dragon's blood —can be used on it.

Other gilding methods

Imitation gold paint and wax gilding should be mentioned. The first has always been looked upon with disdain—and rightly so, because the available material was indeed inferior. Now an excellent product has appeared on the market: Treasure Gold Liquid Leaf, available in better art material stores. When used on small ornaments (like carved details) and placed alongside a genuine gold leaf application (especially when the liquid leaf is burnished), the two can hardly be told apart. The paint does not tarnish, dries quickly, and within an hour or two it can be treated with orange shellac or with the other materials used for antiquing and coloring gilded surfaces.

The second material (produced by the same manufacturer) is Treasure Gold Wax Gilt. It employs a formula which was, to my knowledge, first published in one of my early books; but because wax colors have been used since time immemorial, I cannot claim its invention. It employs a Carnauba wax-resin compound (see Chapter 8) and bronze powder so finely ground that its effect closely resembles that of true gold. Wax Gilt comes in a large assortment of colors; its application does not differ from any other method of waxing; and it can be burnished and treated with shellac or with acrylic patinas. The gold paint, as well as the Wax Gilt, can be used for minor repairs of gilded ornaments, picture frames, and ornamental art objects.

Examples and demonstrations

To reproduce the subtleties of gold applications by means of pictures is impossible. Hence the examples shown serve merely to illustrate particular techniques, rather than render facsimiles of gilded surfaces.

In Color Plate 11, only the left hand portion (reaching as far as the legs of the figurine) is original 18th century. The part to the right, as well as the gilded and raw wood base, are new; but their color and texture conform exactly to the look we know in time-worn antique gilding.

The figurine in Color Plate 12 originally had the color of flesh that, although antique (18th century), appeared rather crude and lacking in interest. To remedy this, the object was covered with silver leaf and then antiqued as described in this chapter.

In Fig. 38 an interesting effect was produced on the plinth. First the surface was covered smoothly with black acrylic paint. Upon drying, an acrylic medium was applied and, while still quite wet, aluminum leaf was placed on it. Lightly tapping with the finger broke it into an irregular pattern. The simulated gold color was produced with a single application of orange shellac.

The plinth in Color Plate 13 is new, but it received a treatment of "antique" silver coated with orange shellac on a black ground, giving it an ancient look. On the star ornaments, the original 18th century gilding was almost completely gone and had to be replaced, then given a dusty patina. Such a patina can be produced by adding umber pigment to thinned acrylic gesso, or by rubbing rottenstone into the surface.

Artificial dust

What does such a patina represent? It simply suggests petrified dust, so common on ancient objects which have not received regular dusting—luckily, perhaps, for a few hundred years of systematic cleaning would have worn out even a sturdy piece of furniture or decor.

This gray wash (or patina) is artificial, of course, but we can endow an object with the "real" stuff with our old reliable rottenstone. This gray, finely divided powder (in fact, a bona fide dust) has the quality of clinging to rough surfaces— especially to hard to reach places, cracks, and crevices.

Whether our patina is applied as liquid paint or powdered rottenstone, if used judiciously it will match the appearance of dust that has been conditioned by atmospheric moisture during a prolonged period and finally hardened to solid matter.

FIGURE 38. *Plinth was covered with black acrylic paint. Upon drying, it was moistened with acrylic polymer medium, which served as adhesive for aluminum leaf. While adhesive was still wet, leaf was broken into irregular pattern by tapping with finger. Aluminum was turned gold by orange shellac.*

4
REPAIRING ANTIQUE WOODEN SCULPTURE AND DECORATIVE OBJECTS

I have discussed the various damages which may befall an ancient object made of wood, with one exception, the infestation of wood worms. The degree of such infestation varies according to the nature of the wood and the climate to which an object has been exposed; but the severity of the damage is not necessarily related to age. I have seen medieval pieces with no worm holes at all and examples less than one hundred years old which were badly affected by the insects.

Dealing with worm damage

Now it should also be noted that many worm holes found in "antiques" are really man-made to suggest venerable age, but their detection should offer no difficulty. As a rule, the manufactured worm hole goes straight down, although it can also be drilled or pricked at an angle. One also reads of cases where such holes have been made by buckshot. But no human hand can produce the bona fide hole which pursues its course in a curved direction, often *parallel* to the surface. (It would appear that the insect, debilitated by its initial effort to penetrate the top surface, prefers to work in a horizontal direction rather than continue digging in depth.) This horizontal direction can be quite shallow or reach a considerable depth; it can also change direction. Another characteristic of a genuine worm hole is its perfectly sharp cut edges—these are never serrated.

To deal with an object thus affected, the damaged areas should first be drenched with an insect killer sprayed from an aerosol can. Next, cover the object closely with plastic wrap, making it airtight, and leave it wrapped for a few days. This will insure that the destructive action of any worms in the wood has been stopped. If wood dust appears next to the object later on, this would indicate that some infestation still remains.

After disinfection, the affected areas (Fig. 39) should be sprayed with Krylon, which penetrates the surface to a certain depth. But to make the honeycombed wood substance solid again, it must be impregnated with acrylic polymer medium. This should be done with a stiff bristle brush. Thus treated, even greatly deteriorated surfaces can be rendered hard and impervious to further harm.

Repairing worm eaten wood

The next two examples illustrate repairs made to ornamental parts of small objects— two postaments serving as supports for sculptured figurines. In Fig. 40, the gilded corner ornament was literally eaten away by wood worms, leaving an empty shell—a jagged fragment of the gilded gesso surface. To repair the damage, the cavity was first filled with quick drying wood putty, stopping about 1/4″ short of the height which the repaired surface would finally reach. Next, white modeling paste was made stiffer by adding dry pigment to it; iron oxide red was mixed with the paste, but any other pigment would have been equally suitable because the surface (to be gilded) was to receive a final layer of the red gilder's clay.

The relative stiffness of the modeling paste made shaping the ornament quite easy. This was accomplished with a modeling tool (Fig. 35). Upon drying, the ornament was painted with red gilder's clay, polished with steel wool, then gilded and covered with orange shellac (Fig. 41).

It should be mentioned that adding dry pigment to the modeling paste impairs its capacity to adhere to the surface. To prevent this from happening, the surface of the putty should be moistened with

FIGURE 39. *Back of Gothic (14th century) figure, badly honeycombed by worms, must be disinfected with insecticide spray, impregnated with acrylic medium.*

FIGURE 40. *Gilded corner ornament of 18th century postament was completely eaten away by worms.*

FIGURE 41. *Shape was modeled with acrylic modeling paste, coated with red gilder's clay, polished with steel wool, gilded, burnished, covered with orange shellac.*

acrylic painting medium before applying the paste.

In Fig. 42, a second postament is seen in the initial stage of repair. The prominent parts that were knocked off in course of time (marked x) were first built up with modeling paste (see closeup in Fig. 43); it was used as it comes from the can, in semi-liquid form. The paste applied to the object was left in a rough state (see arrows) because surface roughness offered a good anchorage for the stiff paste that was finally used on top. Additional applications of paste followed until the proper shape was achieved. Next the forms were painted with red gilder's clay, again polished (this time with steel wool), then gilded and antiqued. In Fig. 44 the object appears fully "recovered," and the added parts cannot be distinguished from those that remained in their original condition.

Restoring wood sculpture: a simple demonstration

The next two examples represent restorations of 16th century Spanish altarpieces. Although (as I have mentioned previously) fragmentary figures often possess their own intrinsic charm, in certain cases they may call for repair. This condition is obvious in Fig. 46. The arm had to be replaced. There was no problem in carving this small object, using the tools in Figs. 35 and 45 and the motor with proper attachments (Fig. 8). The face of the Roman soldier, however, despite its extensive damage, appeared just right and was left untouched.

Not so the missing polychromy. A number of gaps in the surface color can be seen in Fig. 47, both on the figures and on the molding at the bottom. All these created a disturbing effect. The repair of these damaged areas was rather simple. The gaps were filled with acrylic modeling paste

FIGURE 42. *Prominent parts, knocked off by past abuse, were roughly reshaped with acrylic modeling paste (marked X).*

FIGURE 43. *Closeup of repairs (see arrows) in acrylic modeling paste, plus additional applications of the same material.*

FIGURE 44. *Repaired forms were covered with red gilder's clay, polished with steel wool, gilded, antiqued respectively.*

FIGURE 45. *Woodcarving tools.*

FIGURE 46. *Detail from Spanish altarpiece (16th century) in original damaged condition.*

FIGURE 47. *Note gaps in polychromy (surface color). These were filled with acrylic modeling paste (tinted red with iron oxide dry pigment), then gilded or painted.*

turned red by an admixture of iron oxide pigment; these were later gilded or given the appropriate color (Fig. 48). On such small spots, there is no need to use red clay under the gilding or to apply acrylic medium for a better attachment of the rather stiff modeling paste. It is only on heavy, projecting forms where this consideration becomes important.

Originally, most of the relief's surface had been treated in graffito. Hence, after gessoing and gilding, the graffito was done as described in Chapter 3. In making various repairs to gilding, graffiti, and other gaps, every attempt was made to retain the *acceptable* ravages caused by age, and not to go overboard in giving an appearance of newness (see completed restoration, Fig. 49). Within an architectural setting (the relief was part of a large altar, representing a scene from the Calvary), the wear and tear suffered through centuries creates a lively surface that entices our sensibilities and should never be violated. Over-restoration can become just as objectionable as no restoration at all.

Repairing wood sculpture: a more complex demonstration

The problem of restoration proved to be difficult in one of three unified sections, part of a complex altar of the finest design and workmanship (Figs. 50 and 51). Judging from the condition of the panel, a battery of wax candles must have been burning in front of it over a long period of time, causing dessication of the wood. (The wood might also have been insufficiently seasoned when originally used for carving.) In consequence, the heavy gesso coating and gilding have not been able to follow the contraction of the wood, but have buckled in spots, developing a network of severe cracks and detaching from the sup-

FIGURE 48. *Closeup of refinished surface—antique appearance restored.*

FIGURE 49. *Completed restoration retains characteristic signs of age. Collection of the author.*

FIGURE 50. *First steps in restoring section of 16th century altarpiece. Note surface darkened by candle flames, loss of gilding on many spots of surface. On background at left, repairs have begun with modeling paste.*

FIGURE 51. *Damaged areas have been gessoed, gilded, antiqued to conform with aged, undamaged parts. Collection of the author.*

port in many areas. Moreover, the flame of the candles (undoubtedly fanned by a draft) left several burns in the surface of the panel; in addition, their soot incorporated itself into the gilding so firmly that even scraping it with a razor sharp X-acto knife (Fig. 52) proved hopeless.

Tentative steps in the panel's restoration are represented in Fig. 50. Considering the nature and variety of the defects, both red gilder's clay and acrylic modeling paste had to be used. The paste was used to rectify damages that showed some depth, such as holes, cracks, etc.; the clay was used on *all* the sculptured parts. On the large, flat surfaces, the red clay was applied with a palette knife; upon drying, it was well sandpapered. On gilder's clay, sanding and polishing offer no difficulty; not so in the case of the harder modeling paste! The usual gilding followed.

The dotted intaglio pattern at the bottom of the panel, which was almost entirely destroyed, had to be completely redone. Here, after gessoing and gilding, a blunt, 5″ end section of a brush handle served as a pounce for hammering the dots into the gilded gesso surface.

Strangely and unaccountably, some parts of the carving did not suffer any damage at all; much of the ornamentation on the oblong panels, for example, remained in excellent condition, although their gilding darkened as much the rest of the surface.

Before applying a patina on the newly gilded surfaces, some of the gold was rubbed off, thus uncovering the red ground underneath. In this manner, the gilding was initially antiqued. Next, its final color had to be considered. Burnt umber and some ivory black seemed to yield the closest approximation of the original color. A little of these, in dye form, were mixed with white shellac and a little orange shellac to

FIGURE 52. *Left to right: small carving knife, round rasp, three corner file, flat file, woodworking rasp, rasp for working with marble, X-acto knife.*

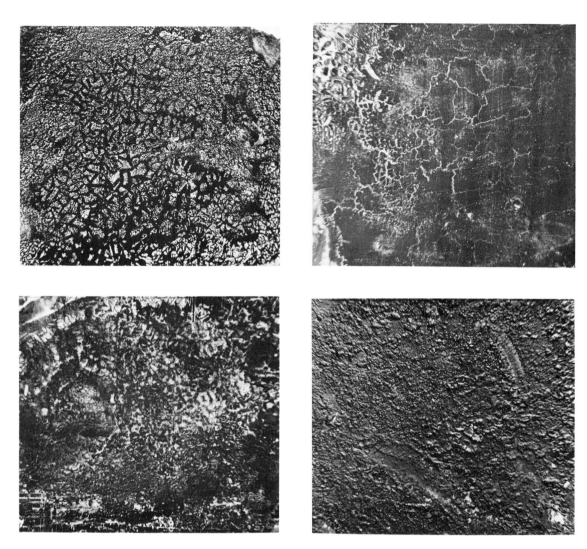

FIGURES 53-56. *Various crackle effects were produced by painting eggwhite-gum Arabic emulsion on surface prepared from asphaltum solution in turpentine, with some wax added, and then exposing to heat. Character of crackle is determined by degree of heat and thickness of underpainting.*

serve as patina. The mixture was applied first with a bristle brush and then a piece of cheesecloth was pressed into the still wet surface. This produced a texture similar to the one seen on the old lusterless gilding. Instead of tinted shellac, the resin-wax compound, mixed with some umber pigment and some black would also have served the purpose. When the patina was dry, the surface was polished with the finest steel wool and then waxed. Rottenstone was finally distributed judiciously to enter the minute cracks, crevices, and nooks.

To repeat, all new additions (Fig. 51) were treated to blend with the original texture of the four hundred year old relief.

Producing artificial corrosion

Thus far, we have been dealing with remedies for all sorts of deterioration in antique wooden objects, plus ways of creating facsimiles of certain characteristic antique appearances. Now I shall discuss a method of producing the corrosion and crackle that make some surfaces look "genuinely" antique.

The problem of achieving that elusive surface quality—which "only time can produce"—is to superimpose two films of paint which possess a certain *incompatibility,* specifically a hard surface on top of a soft one.

Logically, the softest paint is one prepared from wax mixed with dry pigment. First, we shall liquefy a piece of beeswax by placing it in a metal container and subjecting it to heat. An electric hot plate should be used for this purpose. Upon liquefying, the wax-melt should receive about 15% linseed oil, 10% damar picture varnish, and enough dry pigment to form a dense color paste. The paste (which is the same material used in encaustic painting)

must be kept warm and liquid in a hot water bath (double boiler). Because wax paint solidifies rapidly, the surface to which it is applied should be preheated by exposure to a hot plate. If this is not feasible, even the roughest encaustic paint surface can be made smooth by treating it with a palette knife preheated over a flame.

When hardened, the surface should be covered with an emulsion of egg white mixed with gum Arabic in the proportion of 1:1. The egg white, when dry, yields a hard, impervious film—too hard for our purpose—therefore the addition of gum Arabic.

Now the treated surface should be placed near an electric heater or any other source of heat, but not close enough to scorch the emulsion. In no time, the expanding wax paint will cause the superimposed egg white-gum Arabic film to break into a fine crackled net. The thicker the underlying layer and the stronger the heat, the deeper the cracks will form, even to the point of "alligatoring." (The term refers to the pattern we see on an alligator's skin.)

A more delicate crackle can be produced by mixing wax with a thick asphaltum solution. This will result in a black color which, however, can be changed as follows. An addition of titanium white pigment will gray it down considerably, thus allowing the color to be conditioned by adding any other pigment. But if you use iron oxide pigments of great tinting capacity (such as Mars red, for example), graying the asphaltum-wax color is not necessary. The egg white-gum Arabic mixture is then applied and can be used repeatedly in order to achieve the desired result.

The wide variety of possible effects is seen in Figs. 53-56.

A method capable of producing a more drastic crackle effect (Fig. 57) calls for dis-

FIGURE 57. *This effect was produced by coating surface with an asphaltum ground, then with colored dextrin paste. Heating surface produced severe alligatoring. If thinner layer of dextrin paint were used and less heat applied, surface would show only mild scaling.*

solving asphaltum powder in benzene with a small quantity of beeswax added to form a thick paint. This should be applied immediately because the material dries rapidly. The common, so-called white library paste (made of dextrin) should be mixed with any desired pigment and painted on top of the asphaltum surface. Upon drying, subject the surface to heat; this will make the scales of the rapidly forming crackle raise at their borders like little saucers. To reattach them completely, press them down with a piece of paper. The character of the crackle is governed by the thickness of the dextrin paint and the degree of heat used. Now spray the water soluble surface with Krylon fixative and finally cover it with acrylic gel. For further protection, use wax-resin compound or matte picture varnish. Thus treated, the "antique" finish will acquire great permanence.

I should also mention an industrial preparation called Crackle Finish, now available in paint stores as an enamel or lacquer paint. The first can be applied with a brush; the second has to be sprayed over a dry lacquer surface. The thinner the coat, the finer the crackle. The material shrinks as it dries.

Both the methods I have described produce only the alligator type of crackle, which is not necessarily a characteristic of antique polychromy.

Once we have succeeded in crackling and corroding a surface, we can proceed to endow its texture with intriguing effects of glazing or scumbling. The paint used for this purpose can be acrylic, oil, or even watercolor. (To make a water medium go over the wax surface without trickling—or "crawling" as it is called—we shall have to add a trace of detergent.) Now the newly created finish can be protected with wax-resin compound, preferably the Carnauba-copal composition.

Are such techniques likely to produce a crop of forgeries? I was recently visited by the director of the most prominent art auction house in New York. Upon seeing the manuscript of this treatise and the illustration material on my desk, the gentleman showed visible concern. With such a guide at hand, he said, a manufacturer of "antiques" could have a field day. I must admit that I have no such fear. If one buys antiques from an established and respected house, the chance of being deceived is very scant—except in very rare cases where even a hard bitten expert fails to recognize a deception. Being something of an expert in the field, with almost half a century of experience and a great many purchases, I have hardly ever been "taken."

5
RESTORING STONE, TERRACOTTA, AND OTHER STONE-LIKE MATERIALS

Three principal kinds of stone (of the calcium carbonate variety) are used to fashion sculpture and artifacts, and all are closely related in chemical composition: limestone, marble, and alabaster. These differ in crystalline structure, density, and hardness. The last two qualities are responsible for the stone's durability, very important when an object is kept outdoors. The density of the material—that is, the closeness of the grain—accounts for the degree of surface smoothness and gloss that can be achieved through polishing.

Limestone, marble, and alabaster

If the stone displays decorative patterns and/or color, limestone which possesses this characteristic is generally referred to as marble. (Marble is metamorphic rock formed by the action of geologic heat and pressure on limestone.) In its true form, limestone is softer than marble; the color of limetone is uniformly light gray or yellowish, and its surface appears dull and sandy instead of crystalline. But even the hardest marble, when exposed to weathering, becomes grainy, losing its smoothness and gloss; as such, it may become indistinguishable from limestone.

Both these minerals are found in a great many localities in Europe as well as in America, but the best quality comes from Greece. It is still quarried from the mountain Pentelicus near Athens; hence it is called Pentelic. This material has a particular surface lucidity. Carrara marble, also famed for its beauty, comes from the Italian village of the same name; because of its fine crystalline structure, close grain, and uniform white or creamy color, it is much valued as a material for sculpture.

Alabaster is a kind of marble distinguished by a high degree of translucency; it is also much softer than the other two materials and is generally used for small decorative objects rather than for large scale sculpture. When held against strong light, alabaster as thick as $\frac{1}{2}''$ will show translucency. When freshly cut from the rock, it is often snowy white, but it seems to acquire a soft, creamy color with age.

Terracotta

Terracotta is a ceramic clay containing iron oxide; hence its color is generally red. Through the addition of other pigments, this color can be modified. Chemically, terracotta consists of kaolin and silica, and its plastic quality makes it an ideal material for sculpture and pottery. When fired in kilns and left either in its natural state or glazed with various ceramic materials, it acquires considerable hardness and thus becomes very durable.

Cement

Portland or hydraulic cement is obtained by burning limestone and clay in a kiln or furnace. In order to use the material for structural as well as casting purposes, it is mixed with sand or marble dust (in proportions that range from 1:1 to 1:3), and enough water is added to form a dense paste. When precise detail is to be repaired, the mixture should be richer in cement; the 1:1 ratio is considered the richest. Objects cast in this material are referred to as cast stone.

In its natural state, the color is a dull gray; but when colored pigments are added to the mix, any tint can be produced. Mixed with sufficient titanium white, cement can be made perfectly white; after the white is added, the cement can be tinted blue or green with phthalocyanine pigments. A white cement is also available on the market. When red, brown, or black cement is needed, the cement paste (without the titanium white pigment) can be mixed directly with the appropriate Mars pigments.

Raw cement is highly hygroscopic (water absorbing) and therefore should be kept in a dry place, protected from moisture. When well mixed with sand and water, hardened cement offers great resistance to deterioration when kept out of doors. Its specific gravity (hence its density) is greater than any other stone material mentioned here.

One important circumstance should be kept in mind: cement mix becomes unmanageable in a relatively short time (although it may take days to cure thoroughly, depending on the thickness of the mass). However, a small addition of plaster of Paris delays setting. Here is another measure to make the material more amenable to shaping with modeling tools: mix it with acrylic polymer medium instead of water. When attempting to restore marble objects, acrylic medium should be used instead of water.

An excellent product that combines cement and polyvinyl resin is manufactured by the Campbell company under the trade name Top 'n Bond. This cement is mixed with sand and is suitable for repairing limestone objects; because its texture remains rough, Top 'n Bond will not simulate smooth marble surfaces. The material can be worked for a few hours before it sets; depending on atmospheric conditions and the thickness of application, it may take several days for the material to become thoroughly hardened. However, when exposed to heat—sun or artificial heat—its curing is greatly accelerated. Thus a thickness of about $\frac{1}{2}''$ can be well hardened within about six hours.

Acrylic modeling paste

A product that can be easily shaped and which possesses good resistance to weathering, even when kept outdoors for an extended time, is acrylic modeling paste (Liquitex is recommended). It consists of marble dust dispersed in acrylic polymer medium. Because of its white color and slight tinting capacity, the paste can be tinted easily by simply adding dry pigment. When the paste becomes too stiff, thus losing its capacity to adhere to the assigned place, some acrylic medium should be mixed in.

However, working with the paste entails certain difficulties. Although it possesses great plasticity, its tendency to dry quickly at the surface (remaining moist within) makes it difficult to use for repairs of an intricate sculptural nature. When used in a thickness exceeding $1/4''$, the dried paste may fissure at the top; but this is no great problem since the fissures can be covered up or filled when the mass dries.

At any rate, when working with this material, it is best to build it up in stages, applying successive layers about $1/8''$ thick, always allowing the underlying layer to dry well before commencing with the next layer. When hardened, the paste can be cut with a coping saw, filed with wood rasps, sanded and polished to a high gloss with a burnisher.

Plaster of Paris

Finally, plaster of Paris should be mentioned. It is obtained from gypsum (calcium carbonate) dehydrated by burning. When mixed with water to a dense paste, it hardens rapidly and becomes largely water-insoluble. When a small amount of glue size is added to the wet plaster paste, its drying will be materially slowed down, allowing the plaster to be freely molded for one or two hours. Slow setting types of plaster of Paris (with retarding agents added) are also sold ready mixed. The wet paste can be mixed with any desired dry pigment or, when dry, it can be colored with acrylic paint.

Restoring stone statuary and ornaments

This chapter will consider both antique and not-so-antique statuary, for the problems of their restoration are not identical.

Let us first consider Greek, Hellenistic, Roman, and Byzantine sculpture. Very few —if any—of these have come to us undamaged. The specimens we find nowadays in museums may appear with all or most of their original marble in place; but one can safely assume that these are mended, augmented, and generally patched up. This may have been done yesterday, 100 or 500 years ago, or perhaps much earlier. In past times, there were no compunctions about turning fragments of Greek statuary, for example, into complete pieces, dazzling in their apparent newness. (Just remember Thorwaldsen's restoration of the Aegina marbles, now in the Munich Glyptothek.) Only in present day museum practice do we see every new restoration or addition conscientiously registered on the identifying label.

That fragmentary antique pieces often have an intriguing look is an undeniable fact. But this is not always the case. The probing eye of the knowledgeable onlooker must decide whether an existing mutilation constitutes a defacement—whether it should be corrected or left "as found."

It may be unwise to tamper with objects of great or comparatively great antiquity. What happens, however, when an object is less ancient, less valuable? In such objects, disfigurements become esthetically less and less acceptable. A missing nose on a neo-classic object, for example, will surely devalue it to the point of worthlessness and will call for remedial measures. Moreover, works of strictly decorative or ornamental nature lose their appeal when mutilated. (I am well aware that a badly mangled Greek column does not suffer such a loss, but I am also certain that this appeal is a sentimental one, pure and simple.) Therefore, in my opinion, ornaments of every kind should be restored to some degree whenever possible and the patina that they have acquired through the ages should be faithfully reestablished.

Restoring decorative details

Let us start with a few typical examples of repairs. Fig. 58 represents a Corinthian capital made of light brownish-gray marble. Obviously, it must have been kept out of doors during a certain period when its intricate carving was fairly obliterated. In fact, its surface was so weatherbeaten and roughened that it lost its original marble appearance. This condition was the deciding factor in choosing the granular finish of cement for the repair. The mixture consisted of equal parts of cement and marble dust, plus enough acrylic polymer medium to form a paste of suitable consistency for modeling. To match the original color, titanium white, umber, and ochre dry pigments were added to the cement mix; and some more acrylic medium was mixed in because the addition of the pigments made the paste too stiff. Work was done in stages: the forms were built up gradually wherever a thick application was needed, since this could not have been managed easily in one operation (Fig. 59). The only tools used for shaping the cement are seen in Fig. 35: a stylus and a sculptor's modeling tool, both made of wood.

The Renaissance marble plinth (Fig. 60) on which the 8th century head is mounted (Fig. 61) was nicked in several places,

FIGURE 58. *Corinthian marble capital, badly weathered. Collection of the author.*

FIGURE 59. *Same capital repaired with mixture of equal parts cement and marble dust, plus enough acrylic medium to form a paste tinted with titanium white, ochre, umber dry pigments.*

FIGURE 60. *Italian marble pedestal (16th century), badly chipped in several places.*

which made this decorative object quite unsightly. (Not so the highly distorted ancient head, where any restorations would have been prohibitive.) The repair was carried out with modeling paste to which a trace of cadmium yellow was added to make its color blend with that of the plinth. After the additions dried thoroughly, they were polished to a smooth surface, then burnished to a high gloss. Burnishers are seen in Figs. 34 and 35.

Repairing heads

Fig. 62, an outdoor, over life-size, neo-classic head (evidently from the early 19th century) had lost its nose. This accident obviously disfigured the head's profile badly. For the repair, a mixture of acrylic medium, cement, and marble dust was used (Fig. 63). Although the color of the marble was perfectly white, the relatively large quantity of titanium white pigment (needed to overcome the gray color of the cement) made the mixture *too* white and hence had to be toned down with a little umber pigment.

Figs. 64 and 65 are both of Roman origin. In the first, any restoration would have invalidated its particular appeal. An entirely different problem presented itself in the head in Fig. 65; here it appears in its "post-operative" stage. (The head was acquired before this book was conceived, hence no photo of its original condition was made.) Instead of the nose, a concavity originally disfigured the face, and part of the chin was also missing. Restoration appeared mandatory. The nose and the chin were reconstructed (as described in the preceding paragraph), but the lips and other damaged spots were left untouched.

The same consideration prevailed in the replacement of the missing nose in Fig. 66. Here, too, care was taken not to make the

FIGURE 61. *Same pedestal repaired with tinted acrylic modeling paste, polished and burnished (when dry) to high gloss. Byzantine (8th century) head on pedestal was left purposely unrestored. Collection of the author.*

FIGURE 62. *Early 19th century garden figure had become defaced.*

FIGURE 63. *Damage was repaired with mixture of acrylic medium, cement, marble dust, titanium white and umber dry pigments. Collection of the author.*

FIGURE 64. *Roman marble head (Republican Period) was left unrestored, since original damaged condition did not detract from esthetic appeal. Collection of the author.*

FIGURE 65. *Another Roman marble head (1st century, A.D.) was found minus its nose and part of chin. Shown here repaired with mixture of acrylic medium, marble dust, cement, dry pigments. Lips and other damages were left untouched. Collection of the author.*

FIGURE 66. *Texture of repaired nose of Roman head conforms to rest of original pitted marble surface (see complete bust in Fig. 67). Repair was made with cement, marble dust.*

FIGURE 67. *Note rough texture of complete bust and compare with repaired head in Fig. 58. Modeling of repaired portions should be consistent with original texture of object. Collection of the author.*

addition differ in texture from the rest of the marble surface, which was quite pitted (Fig. 67).

Fig. 68 represents an 18th century Venetian sculpture made of Istrian marble or limestone; here it is difficult to establish a borderline between these closely related materials. In Fig. 69, the figure is still in Venice, its texture enhanced by the growth of lichen and algae that quickly vanished in the unfavorable climate of New York to which it was moved. In Fig. 69, the weird look of the cavernous nose was improved through a slight "cosmetic" operation, accomplished with acrylic modeling paste tinted with a trace of ivory black and burnt umber dry pigment.

Fig. 70 represents a limestone head of Roman origin from the 4th century A.D. Because it showed considerable deterioration, the repair was made with Top 'n Bond cement, ideally suited for work on rough limestone surfaces. To match the color of the object, a small quantity of titanium white dry pigment was added to the cement mix. As verified by examining the repaired head (Fig. 71) under a magnifying glass, an identical texture prevails on the original and added parts—the nose, chin, and lower lip.

The object in Color Plate 14 was made of terracotta. The original color of the unpainted clay was red. The iron oxide and haematite oxide content of the clay probably account for the extraordinary hardness of the material. The head and hair were originally painted in tempera or oil color that became flaky here and there. This was left untouched, but the head was broken at the neck and that is where the rather extensive addition was made. Acrylic modeling paste has proven the ideal material for this purpose. It was mixed with an iron oxide pigment—which was really superfluous

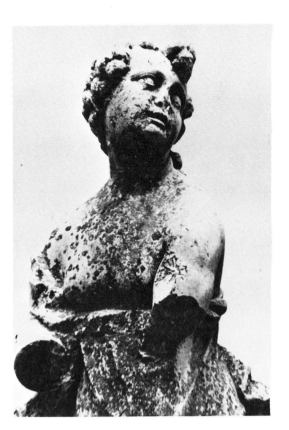

FIGURE 68. *Venetian sculpture of Istrian marble (18th century) had broken nose, was covered with algae, lichen while in Venice.*

FIGURE 69. *Damage was repaired with acrylic modeling paste tinted lightly with ivory black, burnt umber dry pigment; algae, lichen disappeared with change of climate from Venice to New York. Collection of the author.*

FIGURE 70. *Roman limestone head (4th century, A.D.) was heavily weathered, missing parts of nose, chin, lower lip.*

FIGURE 71. *Head was repaired with Top 'n Bond cement which conforms with rough limestone texture. Color was modified by titanium white dry pigment to match color of original stone. Collection of the author.*

since the surface was to be painted eventually. However, it was interesting to observe that the configuration and color of the modeling paste were indistinguishable from the original material. Finally the coloring of the surface was done with the acrylic material—Liquitex gesso mixed with red oxide and a trace of ochre pigment.

In making additions with modeling paste, remember that unless it is sufficiently wet and the surface favorable for attachment (that is, of adequate width and roughness), the added part will adhere poorly. The following measure will strengthen the bond. When superficially dry—that is, not thoroughly hardened—the *entire addition* should be removed; in this condition it will come off easily. Next, it should be glued on at once with white synthetic glue or acrylic polymer medium.

Patinas on stone

The patina of ancient marbles does not result from any changes in the chemical composition of the material; it is simply foreign matter attached to the stone. Once marble or limestone is stained, cleaning may prove difficult because the stone is porous and may easily absorb foreign matter that imparts its own color to the material. Acids should not be used because they disintegrate the stone without producing the desired patina.

On marble or limestone surfaces, how can one produce an artificial patina? The rougher the surface, the more easily it can be stained. On limestone, even a highly diluted acrylic paint will work well; but on marble, the use of dyes is preferable. Some of the commonest dyes are tea, coffee, iodine, and mercurochrome. For gray coloring, tannic acid mixed with one of our iron compounds (such as iron chloride, ferric nitrate, or iron sulphate) will yield

the desired result. However, a patina produced in this manner will obviously not penetrate the surface to the depth found in stone that has been buried underground for a great length of time.

To clean stone, washing with soap and water, plus some ammonia is all one can do. Cleaning stone that has been soiled through exposure to outdoor conditions can be done with carbon tetrachloride and 10% benzene. (For safety, work in a well ventilated area.) Upon drying, the stone can be impregnated with a thin mixture of paraffin or beeswax. To make this salve penetrate the surface, the stone should be heated with an electric heater. A more effective method for driving the impregnating liquid into the surface is to use a hot air blower such as employed for drying hair.

Certain kinds of stains cannot be washed away effectively—but cleaning old marbles of their original patina is as prohibitive as removing the patina of an ancient bronze. Nearly any discoloration on antique marbles, once it becomes incorporated into the stone texture, should be left alone. If ordinary cleaning (as suggested above) proves ineffective, we may accept the patina to be genuine; as such, it should be looked upon as inviolate.

We sometimes see Roman marbles whose hair and face differ in tone. Since multicolored marbles were not used on figural objects, the only conclusion we can draw is that the coloring was achieved by artificial means. We know that the Greek sculptors colored their marbles with pigment-beeswax compounds; the polychromy of the Romans must have been produced by an identical operation. But colored wax does not last over centuries—except in rare cases when the object has been sheltered throughout its entire existence—so we must

FIGURE 72. *Marble head had been submerged in a Dutch channel for centuries, acquiring unsightly black color which could not be removed without marring the surface. Color was modified by patina of raw green earth dry pigment dispersed in water, rubbed into rough stone surface. Collection of the author.*

assume that the polychromy is more recent than the marble.

An interesting problem arose in handling the head seen in Fig. 72. It was retrieved from a canal in Delft, Holland, where it lay buried among the debris of a house destroyed in the 17th century. The head, obviously fashioned in the Greek manner, does not impress me as either Greek or Roman, but rather of Baroque origin. When found, it was covered by a black tarry substance, the removal of which, by means of chemicals, proved impossible. The black coloring *could* have been scraped off the marble, but such an operation undoubtedly would have left an unfavorable effect. Since the prevailing blackish color did not enhance the object's appearance, the head was covered with a solution of raw green earth pigment mixed with water. When this patina dried, it was rubbed off with wet rags, allowing the pigment to remain—chiefly in the rough stone surface and in hard to reach depressions, thus softening the effect of the black matter that permeated its texture.

6

TREATING METALS

Let us examine the nature of the metals that go into the making of art objects and artifacts.

Gold—the most precious—does not tarnish. However, if alloyed with much copper and/or silver, or if the gold contains some impurities (as is the case in ancient objects made of this material) it does show changes in color. Of course, we are unlikely to deal with objects made of pure gold. And gold leaf applications have already received close attention in Chapter 3. The other precious metal, silver, whether in its pure form or alloyed with copper or other base metals, does tarnish readily when exposed to air.

But our chief interest will center not on gold or silver, but on the most common metals used in decorative objects: copper, brass, and bronze.

Copper is very sensitive to sulphur and oxygen, especially when exposed to moist air. When buried in damp, salty soil, it loses its metallic appearance; it develops a bluish or greenish incrustation corresponding to the minerals, azurite and malachite.

Brass is an alloy of copper and zinc, while bronze is an alloy of copper and tin; bronze is more resistant to corrosion. Ancient bronze often contains lead and other metals. When bronze is buried in salty soil, chlorides form incrustations that may result in progressive corrosion known as "bronze disease," a condition often difficult to arrest.

It is interesting that the ancient bronze horses placed on the facade of St. Mark's in Venice—originally carried away by the Byzantines from Rome, then stolen during the sack of Constantinople in 1204 by the Crusaders, then removed by Napoleon to Paris and finally returned after his fall—are affected by bronze disease. This disintegration is not the result of all these vicissitudes, nor of burial underground, but

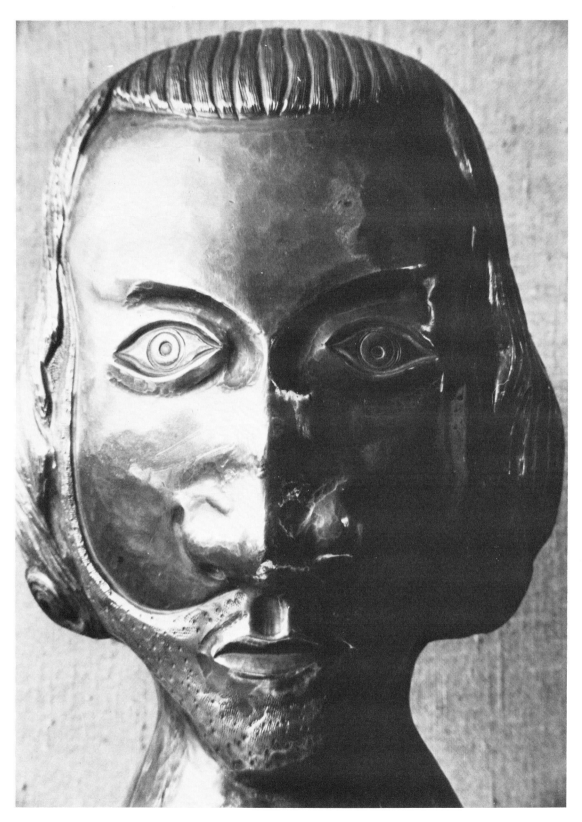

FIGURE 73. *Silver head (age undetermined) was darkened with weak liver of sulphur solution. Prominent parts were polished clean, allowing dark patina to remain in recessed areas. Collection of the author.*

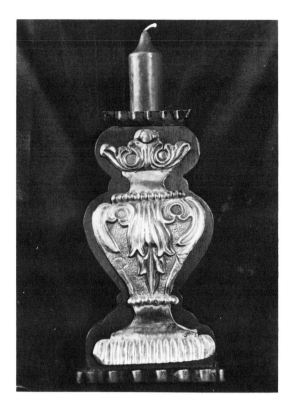

FIGURE 74. *Sicilian mirror frame (17th century) was darkened with liver of sulphur solution. Raised areas were polished to accentuate prominent parts of object. Collection of the author.*

FIGURE 75. *Silver ornament (Austrian, 18th century) was patined with liver of sulphur solution; prominent areas were polished and recessed areas left dark to throw decorative design into relief.*

simply came about through exposure to the salty air of the lagoon city. The only cure for this condition is neutralization (not always successful) of the chlorides in the body of the bronze.

In short, one must understand that the patinas on metals are nonmetallic. They are made up of chemical compounds, oxides, carbonates, chlorides, etc.

Pewter should also be mentioned. It is an alloy of lead and tin. The harder the pewter, the more tin it contains. But in the modern alloy, lead is usually absent; instead, modern pewter contains antimony and sometimes copper as an additive to tin.

Last, there is the lowly iron. When handling this metal, we have only two concerns: to free it from rust, or to induce corrosion, depending upon our requirements.

Shiny finish or patina?

No doubt, there is a justified desire to have one's silver dishes, brass candleholders, and copper pots radiantly bright. But this shiny condition will not make other objects of decorative art more acceptable from an esthetic point of view. In many cases, a fine patina is not only texturally and coloristically attractive, but it invariably enhances the market value of an object, especially when made of bronze.

In Figs. 73-75, we see three antique objects made of silver. To emphasize their decorative pattern, the protruding surfaces were shined, while the lower surfaces forming the background are darker; that is, the background areas remained tarnished, thus enhancing the highlights of the prominent pattern. To keep these shined up—crevices, indentations, and all—would deprive the objects of their textural appeal.

Or take the "ancient" vases in Figs. 76 and 77. What visual attraction would these offer when polished to their best

FIGURE 76. *These are not Persian relics recovered from an ancient tomb, but inexpensive contemporary copper jugs patined and incrusted with various corrosive chemicals.*

FIGURE 77. *Another inexpensive contemporary copper pitcher, patined and incrusted.*

coppery sheen? Or can you imagine a bronze or brass statuette, antique or new, aglitter in polished yellow? Now, a shiny door knob looks fine on a New England style cottage (or even on a Georgian mansion), but one may wish to have it well patined in other surroundings.

As a general rule, ancient objects should carry the patina of age; should this be lost—the oldest of bronze, if still healthy, *can* be deprived of its outer skin—the patina should be recreated. The means of recreating a patina, I might add, need not necessarily be called artificial. In point of fact, the chemical processes used for this purpose do occur in nature, although their effects become manifest gradually, over many decades or even centuries.

Two kinds of patinas

Ancient (and not so ancient) objects made of copper or bronze show two principal patinas: relatively smooth surfaces acquired during the natural course of oxidation above ground, and rough, incrusted surfaces that have aged while buried underground.

The first, it goes without saying, do not have incrustations. The darkening of the originally yellowish color (due to oxidation above ground) provides these objects with a light to dark brown patina. It is a fact that the dark colors seen on statuary in museums were induced artificially by the sculptors—the raw, glistening bronze is not attractive. Neither is the black color, so characteristic of Pompeian bronzes, for example, that was brought about by the hot ashes which covered them after the eruption of Vesuvius. Whatever its color, antique statuary that was not buried or exposed to weather possesses a smooth surface free from corrosion of any kind.

This is not the case with ancient objects that were found underground, for under such conditions the metals tend to revert to minerals. Some of these mineral incrustations may be stable; others may not, such as the bronze disease previously mentioned. It has been accepted that the presence of chlorides within the metallic bodies is responsible for this condition.

Patining is an art

In books on sculpture, one finds many recipes for patination of bronze objects, and many of these formulas (as well as the unwritten formulas) have been tested by the author. The tests were often inconclusive, perhaps because the original effects produced by time and nature were more or less accidental—the patinas produced by Mother Nature are capricious in the extreme.

Granted, only a scientifically trained metallurgist can categorize this or that chemical reaction and explain phenomena which are mysterious to the unscientific mind. This unscientific audience includes this author and presumably most of his readers. But notwithstanding the limited knowledge of the nonscientist, the imaginative craftsman can go far afield in achieving remarkable results and endowing metals with the most intriguing patinas. For the crux of the matter is this: patination is an art—no hard and fast rules can be devised. The effectiveness of color and texture depend to a large extent on the ingenuity of the craftsman.

Factors governing color and texture

Four factors govern the color and texture you are able to produce by the patining methods described here:

(1) The nature of the alloys that went into the original production of the specific

metal used to make the object.

(2) The original condition of the surface. Is it smooth, rough, or pitted? Is it free from oxidation? Or does it evidence traces of some existing patina?

(3) The length of exposure to the acids you choose to use and the sequence of exposures.

(4) The length of exposure to heat and the degree of heat you use in patining the object.

All these conditions apply to both categories of patination: to smooth, polished surfaces, as well as incrusted surfaces.

Treating silver objects

As we have all experienced, silver becomes tarnished when exposed to air; depending on its constituent alloys, the color becomes more or less darkened, sometimes acquiring a yellowish cast. Removing tarnish offers no problems at all—simply wash with a detergent and some ammonia, or use any one of the available commercial cleaning agents. Cleaning can also be done with a paste made of chalk moistened with methyl alcohol (methanol) and a few drops of ammonia. There is also on the market a specially prepared cloth for giving silver a high polish. Black, tough surface film, usually formed on old silver with a high copper content, can be eliminated with a 5% solution of sulphuric acid.

I have stated that an occasion may arise when it may seem desirable to stain an object made of silver. Such a treatment may be suitable on certain objects of decor such as those in Figs. 73-75. Here, to emphasize the pattern and thus give plasticity to the protruding elements of the ornamentation, the depressed background areas should be darkened. Liver of sulphur (potassium sulphate) is the best agent for this purpose.

A solution prepared from a piece of liver of sulphur the size of a small bean, dissolved in three tablespoonfuls of water, will cause rapid staining of the silver. The liquid should be applied to the appropriate areas with a round, well pointed sable brush. If the oxidation develops to a greater degree than desired, it can be weakened by partial cleaning, as suggested above. When the forms of an object are complex, it is best to stain it all, and then work with the cleaning agent on the prominent parts, leaving the oxidation only in the declivities of the surface.

When the final distribution of light and dark effects has been achieved to one's satisfaction, the finish can be protected by a spray (such as Krylon) which will inhibit further oxidation. Before using the spray, the object must be meticulously cleaned to eliminate any fatty residue. Washing with soap and water will accomplish this.

Treating copper and its alloys

As mentioned, the principal copper alloys contain tin and zinc; in the first case we speak of bronze, in the second of brass. Of course, copper has been used in more or less pure form, chiefly for making vessels, ornamental or utilitarian, rather than for casting statuary. However, in whatever form copper may appear—pure or alloyed— patination will be essentially the same, although the reaction of pure copper to acids will be much more rapid than the reaction of bronze or brass.

The color produced on pure copper will not always be identical with the color produced on alloyed metals. For example, when copper is acted upon by a concentrated solution of liver of sulphur (one lump, the size of a small bean, dissolved in an ounce of water), it will turn dark brown instantly even when cold; whereas bronze or brass will require heating to produce similar effects.

Patining technique

The method of heating a metal object and applying the corrosive chemicals is quite simple. Place the object on a few bricks, a cinder block, or some other surface which is non-flammable. Remove all flammable objects from the immediate area. Then you may begin by applying heat and follow with the chemicals; or you may apply the chemicals first, and follow with heat.

Simply play the flame of the propane torch or Bunsen burner (Figs. 6 and 7) on the metal object, moving the flame over the surface until all parts are evenly heated. When a few drops of water, flicked onto the surface, bubble and sizzle away, the metal is hot enough for most purposes.

Apply the liquid chemicals with an old brush (useless for any other purpose), using a dabbing, tapping motion, rather than long strokes. Keep pulling the brush away, applying the flame intermittently as you work, if you wish to keep the metal hot for repeated applications of chemicals.

The chemicals will evaporate as soon as they hit the hot metal, but you cannot precisely judge the final color until the object cools. How much heat or corrosive chemical to apply—and for how long—is a matter of experience. It is wise to experiment on metal scraps before you try this technique on an object of value. One other pointer: mix your chemicals in paper throwaway cups which you can dispose of after use— and do not throw unused chemicals down the sink, but return them to bottles, carefully labeled.

Brushing on the acids and exposure to heat (or flame) is not always a one phase operation; repeated applications of chemicals and heating are often required to attain the desired color. The more intense the

heat, such as occurs when exposing the object directly to flame, the darker (and sometimes the lighter) will be its color. Furthermore, different areas of the same object can receive different treatment, depending on the inventiveness of the craftsman.

To make a color become part of the metal—not just loosely attached to it— subjection to heat, or still better flame, is often helpful. This is especially true with the incrustations which we shall presently discuss because these, in contrast to effects produced with chemicals like potassium sulphate and ferric nitrate, often possess appreciable thickness. Such finished surfaces can be protected with Krylon spray and/or waxed. The initially fragile coloring and incrustations seem to become more solid in time.

Light brown, brown-black, and black effects

These are the colors commonly found on bronzes from classical times to the present, as seen in museum collections. They are also the colors most easily attained. For light brown to burnt siena color effects, all you need to do is to heat the object (for heating equipment, see Figs. 6 and 7) and brush on ferric sulphate (one tsp. powder to 1 oz. water). For dark browns and rich brown-blacks, potassium sulphate solution (liver of sulphur) should be used on the heated metal surface.

Finishing touches

After achieving the proper color and washing the object well in running water, you can apply finishing touches by highlighting and polishing the object with wax.

Highlighting can be done first with the finest steel wool or polishing cloth, used on the prominent surfaces and contours. For example, take a bronze head; its dark color can be enlivened by rubbing off some of the patina from the bridge and tip of the nose, the contours of the eyelids, the mouth, top of the hair—in short from all the places where the dark, antique bronze would show glints of lighter color appearing from within. On old objects, these glints or highlights are due to years of dusting by assiduous domestics.

Finally, a light coat of wax will give the object a bright glow. Bronze foundries generally use paraffin.

Other colors and incrustations

The following formulas will yield the other principal colors. The object must be well oxidized before applying the patina. The simplest method of oxidation is to expose the object to the weather until the metal darkens. This should take a few weeks. Brushing on copper sulphate or a solution of 1 tsp. salt and 4 oz. vinegar will have the same effect.

Greenish-bluish effects: 1 oz. copper carbonate, ½ oz. copper sulphate, ¼ oz. ammonium chloride, ¼ oz. acetic acid (glacial), 6 oz. water. Repeated applications, alternated with light heating, are necessary.

Greenish tones: 1 oz. copper nitrate, 1 oz. ammonium chloride, 1 oz. calcium chloride, 6 oz. water. Heat lightly after application. Surface should be prestained with some acid to a darker color (see earlier section on browns).

Crusty, grayish-brown patina: prestain surface with liver of sulphur and burn in with flame. Sprinkle with mixture of 1 oz. ammonium chloride, 6 oz. water. Burn with flame after application and repeat the process several times.

Variegated light colors: ½ oz. copper nitrate, ½ oz. ammonium sulphate, ½ oz.

calcium chloride, 1 pt. water. Heat lightly before application.

Deeply embedded brown and bluish-green colors: first, treat the metal with the propane torch until it turns red. Then dip it into sulphuric acid. Next, the metal should be well washed, heated again to a red color, and dipped into nitric acid. Handle these acids with extreme caution.

Another experiment involved the following successive operations on a single piece of copper previously stained dark brown with ferric nitrate. (1) Apply copper acetate, then burn. Color: light yellowish-green. (2) Apply copper acetate, then burn. Color: dark green. (3) Apply copper sulphate, then burn. Color: light greenish-gray. (4) Apply copper sulphate; heat but do not burn, and let dry. Color: light cerulean blue. The less heat used, the deeper the color.

A commercial formula for blue-green

Have you ever been fascinated by the bluish-green color seen on the domes of ancient churches? These were covered with copper (in contrast to early Medieval edifices which used lead for roofing) and this enchanting color is due to the formation of copper carbonate on the metallic surface. Known as vert antique, a very close associate of malachite and azurite, it is often seen in mineral form as marble veneer used for decorations in precious surroundings.

I have given several formulas for obtaining bluish-green patinas on copper alloys, but for a most uniformly distributed copper green, obtained without the aid of heating, the formula devised by the David Litter Laboratories (116 East 16th Street, New York, New York 10003) is undoubtedly the easiest to apply. It consists of a patinator called Component A, which is a thick green solution (brand name: Incra Patine No. 60b), and Component B, which is concentrated (37%) hydrochloric acid, a very corrosive liquid to be handled with great caution (do not substitute muriatic acid, an impure and weaker form).

The formula for Incra Patine (No. 60b) is as follows: 7 oz. copper sulphate; 4 oz. ammonium sulphate; 6 oz. lithium chloride; 0.4 oz. sodium dichromate; 23 oz. Ben-A-Gel EW (6%) (a proprietary formula of the above mentioned laboratories); 12.5 oz. water. I am registering the ingredients although I assume that an amateur will not wish to compound them. As mentioned, the formula can be obtained ready-mixed. (Incidentally, Ben-A-Gel EW is nothing but a thickening agent, small percentages of which have the capacity of turning water into a gel, when incorporated by high speed stirring; the task of this gel is to keep the surface moist for several hours.)

The ratio between Component A and hydrochloric acid, as given by the laboratories, is 5.6 to 1 by volume. It would seem to me that this ratio represents the minimum quantity of acid used for effective action; I have doubled the ratio and obtained equally good results. However, it appears that a considerable increase of the acid produces a color that is paler and more gray green.

After adding Component B (the acid) to Component A in a glass container and shaking the mixture vigorously, it is ready to be applied by means of a nylon brush, whose metal ferrule should be protected from corrosion by a coating of asphaltum solution. The patinator works best on moderately oxidized (weathered outdoors or treated with salt and vinegar) copper which should be a dark reddish-brown color. Heavily oxidized (blackened) copper gives a somewhat dull, grayish initial color that gradually improves with age, however. Before treating, it is important to free the metal from all previous coatings, grease, etc.; wash thoroughly with a detergent, every trace of which should be rinsed away.

The patina begins to develop quickly on application and increases in intensity during the first few days. Its color is originally an intense green, but on exposure gradually changes to a lighter bluish-green, more closely resembling a natural patina (Color Plate 16). However, on some qualities of copper, bluish-green colors will appear not in a uniform layer, but intermixed with green spots, giving the object a blotchy antique look, almost indistinguishable from authentic pieces found underground. Such experiences illustrate the fact that effects achieved through patination are often capricious (see Color Plate 15).

Apply only one coat of this formula; successive applications are ineffectual. Once attained, the finish can be protected by spraying the object with Krylon and/or coating it with wax-resin compound.

A note on incrustations

Now a word on the problem of incrustations. When produced on "healthy" (that is, smooth) metal, these patinas will lack the roughened character seen on genuine objects; that is, the metal will not be pitted as in Fig. 77. To achieve this, it is necessary to subject the metal to the aquatint process— used in etching the copper plates from which prints are made.

For this purpose, we shall sprinkle rosin with our fingers over the metallic surface. When lightly heated, the rosin attaches itself to the metal; avoid overheating, which makes the rosin particles fuse into a solid film, preventing the acid from working between the particles.

Next, subject the surface to the action of the acid. We could use the rapidly working nitric acid (1:2 or 1:3 in water) or the much weaker iron chloride (1:4 in water). Nitric acid will have to be applied with an eyedropper or a wad of cotton tied to a stick because a bristle or nylon brush will disintegrate. To produce a sufficiently deep "bite" with iron chloride, we shall have to submerge the object in the acid for about an hour; this can hardly be done with statuary, but small metal objects, flat trays, or reliefs can be put in the acid bath. An acid proof tray, made of glass or plastic, can be used for this purpose.

It should be mentioned that nitric acid—unlike iron chloride, which is rather harmless to the skin and respiratory system—is extremely corrosive and breathing its fumes is hazardous to one's health. Nitric acid should be used with caution and in a well ventilated room.

Other experiments

A variety of solutions were made by dissolving a number of copper compounds in the ratio of 1:6 in water. Copper sulphate, copper nitrate, copper acetate, etc. were used on separate pieces of bronze and brass. Each of these was heated prior to treatment with the acids. Copper sulphate turned green-gray and similar coloristic effects were produced with all the other copper compounds. Every one of the metal specimens was then treated in spots and at random with a different copper compound, as well as potassium sulphate and sulphuric acid. The range of effects produced is seen in Color Plate 15.

Strangely, in all my research among published formulas, I did not discover the simple method that employs iron chloride dissolved 1:4 in water. My experiment proceeded as follows.

I saturated a piece of flannel with the liquid and wrapped it tightly around a copper vase, which was kept overnight in a plastic bag. An intriguing yellow-green and brown patina developed. The object can be left in this condition or further treated with one of our chlorides, sulphates, or carbonates. Wetting the surface with acetic acid also brings marked improvement and waxing, of course, will strengthen the attachment of the patina and deepen the color scheme.

It is worth remembering that iron chloride produced grass-green effects of particular brilliance. For strong greens, this acid is especially effective.

An intense blue can be developed by applying a solution of ammonium chloride and water (1:4) to the metal and then exposing the object to acetic acid fumes. The object is placed in a plastic bag with a small open container of glacial acetic acid and the bag is well closed to prevent the fumes from escaping. The acid should not be in direct contact with the metal and the bag should contain a certain amount of air since oxygen is required for the process. In a matter of hours, a deep Prussian blue or sky blue will appear. The same treatment can be given to surfaces previously patined with a variety of other chemicals. Bluish nuances will most often result.

See Color Plate 16 for other possibilities.

Producing natural incrustations

I have described incrustations produced by subjecting objects first to the aquatint process before treating them for color. Now incrustations can also be produced by "natural" means. The following example illustrates this.

A copper vase was buried underground (to a depth of about 10") and the earth around it was saturated with a solution of copper sulphate and water (1:6). After three weeks, when the object was disinterred, a strong blue color enveloped it, but the attachment was poor. Next, the vase was re-buried and the earth was wetted with acetic acid and mixed with a generous amount of salt. When I removed the object after three more weeks, it was partially covered with a light blue-green patina which adhered well. Some bare spots of the metal showed a beautiful, almost vermilion colored surface, and on much of the remaining surface the blue earth formed a barnacle-like incrustation so tough that it could only be removed by scraping with a knife.

Your first experiments with patinas

For convenience, I should like to summarize the roles played by the principal chemicals mentioned in this chapter.

Calcium chloride, iron chloride, sal ammoniac, and copper carbonate belong to the green family. Copper nitrate, copper sulphate, and acetic acid fall into the blue range. Ferric nitrate and liver of sulphur are in a category by themselves: the first produces rich, glowing browns most effective in connection with greens; the second will be called into action for brown to black effects.

Moreover, radically different patina colors will result when you apply the very same mixture of chemicals to clean metallic surfaces and to previously stained surfaces. Different effects will be achieved by changing the quantitative relation of the chemicals. And different colors will develop when you subject the metal to heat (or flame), or when you allow the chemicals to act on a cold surface. The depth of many colors will be enhanced by treating the object with beeswax; however, some light grayish tones may disappear entirely when waxed. Remember that many fragile patinas become quite solid in time.

Because patinas offer endless possibilities, I suggest that the amateur employ the limited number of chemicals enumerated above. He should experiment in a systematic way and make careful notes on the various phases of his operations to arrive at fairly foolproof methods that suit his purposes.

Removing a Patina

You may wish to remove an unsightly patina from an object. If the incrustation is not ancient, the cleaning can be done effortlessly by immersing in diluted sulphuric acid (about 5%). In stubborn cases, diluted nitric acid will prove effective.

Formulas developed by Walter Domes

The following material was presented to me for publication by Mr. Walter Domes of Vienna. His extensive knowledge of the metallic composition of archeological finds has made him one of the foremost experts in this field. Some of Mr. Domes' formulas for patination approximate those I have used, while some lead to excellent results deviating from methods I have described. There is obviously considerable latitude in bringing about comparable results.

(1) In contrast to the patinas which are promoted by applying heat or flame to the object, Mr. Domes recommends those brought about by exposing the previously oxidized object to acids and air drying. The advantage of this technique is that it can be spread over a longer period, which allows the patina to become more durable and natural looking.

A gray-green patina, on copper as well as bronze, can be achieved by suspending the object (previously treated with acids and then thoroughly washed) above a vessel containing a solution of sal ammoniac and acetic acid, thus exposing it to the fumes of these chemicals. This type of patina is fairly firm; however, the superficial layer of the patina should be carefully rubbed off before repeating the treatment in order to strengthen its adhesion still further.

(2) Another procedure calls for dissolving 1 oz. copper nitrate in 4 oz. warm water; a little methanol can be added. A soft rag (or a piece of felt) should be drenched in the solution. Next, a brush should be rubbed against the wet rag and then dabbed onto the surface of the object. It is important not to leave any wet spots, Slowly, through the action of the copper nitrate, a blue-green color starts to develop. This procedure must be repeated until the color becomes uniform.

(3) A greater variety of effects can be achieved by using more elaborate techniques. After treating the object as described above, it is cautiously warmed over low heat until the green layer turns black. Now the loose particles are rubbed off and the piece is again exposed alternately to the acid and then to low heat again and again— this time low enough not to make it turn black. The less heat is used, the more blue-green will the color become. When dabbing with the solution is continued and the heat is increased, the patina turns yellow-green to brown-green. After this treatment, if the object is submerged briefly in an alkaline (soda) solution, a blue-green to deep blue patina will develop. This procedure can also be applied to brass, but the metal must first be turned black by means of iron chloride (not liver of sulphur).

An especially fine patina can be produced if, between successive dabbings, the object is treated with hydrogen peroxide. This first changes the color of the patina to brown; but after repeated moistening with thinned copper nitrate solution, the color turns back to green. At first, one part of the (30%) hydrogen peroxide solution should be diluted with four parts of water; each successive application should be thinned even more, until only pure water is used. The advantage of this is that the object retains —as it would with the genuine antique patina—its brown undertones. Furthermore, the incrustation is more firmly attached to the underlying metal, and many more nuances of coloring can be obtained.

It should be mentioned that the slower the treatment, the more effective and durable the incrustation. Also, when coloring bronze, the copper nitrate solution should receive an equal addition of table salt.

(4) Another formulation for patining bronze is: $\frac{1}{3}$ oz. copper nitrate, $\frac{1}{3}$ oz. copper chloride, 1 oz. zinc sulphate, $\frac{3}{4}$ oz. calcium chloride, $\frac{1}{2}$ oz. mercury chloride, 1 qt. water.

(5) For brass: $\frac{2}{3}$ oz. copper nitrate, 1 oz. zinc sulphate, 1 oz. mercury sulphate, 1 qt. water, and a small addition of vinegar.

(6) A so-called Pompeian green (black-green) coloration can be obtained by brushing the following compound on the object: 4 oz. water, $3\frac{1}{2}$ oz. copper nitrate, plus as much concentrated ammonia water as needed to turn the solution a deep blue. Add 15 oz. 6% acetic acid and $3\frac{1}{2}$ oz. ammonium chloride.

(7) Another formula is made up of 1 pt. water, 2 to 5 oz. sal ammoniac, 3 to 5 oz. ammonium carbonate. This compound is applied to the object repeatedly until the shade of the foundation tint is satisfactory. The solution must always become dry on the object before dabbing on a fresh application. Now any of the patina that has failed to attach itself to the metal should be rubbed off, and the dabbing and drying process

repeated until the desired color has been achieved.

(8) A "natural" patina can be obtained by still another process, but this one demands more time and patience because here the effects are slow in coming. The formula calls for 3 oz. ammonium sulphate, 1 tsp. copper sulphate, 3 tsp. ammonia water (concentrated). The solution is brushed on thinly, air dried, and then repeated until the desired effect materializes.

Domes' observations on patining

Walter Domes made the following general observations about the action of different patining solutions.

It should be noted that changing the weight relationships of the chemicals will produce variations in coloring.

The treatment of copper and bronze, as well as brass, with diluted acetic acid results in a bright green which turns blue when immersed in carbonic acid.

Copper nitrate is also an excellent agent for "pickling"—that is, pre-staining. In some cases, cooking salt can be used for this purpose.

Ammonium butyrate is a fast working medium. It produces a blue-green hue which is very durable.

Ammonium nitrate, used as a foundation, increases the durability of the patina enormously, and is altogether a great help in the preparation of the patina. Subsequent treatment with diluted hydrogen peroxide is recommended.

The slower the development of a patina, the more genuine its appearance and the better its adhesion. It is also important to apply the solutions thinly and allow them to work slowly into the surface. The rule is never to use concentrated solutions.

Non-adhering spots should be wiped or rubbed off carefully and gone over again.

Before making a new application, it is well to polish the dry object gently with a piece of soft material until the surface acquires a faint shine.

Nitrates work rapidly and they yield good colors, but careful control of heating plays a decisive role.

Traces of old oxides should never be removed before the new patina is applied. These brown and black nuances are the best foundation for further coloration.

Methods of forgers

Patination is an art and its facets are many. In fact, for the sake of simplicity, not all have thus far been described. Domes recounts two methods used successfully by some ingenious forgers.

In one case, the object, made of bronze or copper, was placed inside a freshly caught fish, and then buried underground. While the fish decayed, it developed gases which, combined with the acid of the soil, had an oxidizing effect on the metal. After all the organic matter had disintegrated, the object, which had now acquired a bright green color, was washed and submerged in soda water until the patina turned blue. To enhance the durability of the surface coating, the object was deposited for a whole year in a wine cellar, where the fermenting gases produced a patina that could not have been distinguished from one developed through centuries.

Another "famous" forger used the following method. With the help of acids, he first produced a very rough surface. (I described this process of aquatint etching earlier in this chapter.) Such surface characteristics are, as I pointed out, very conducive to further treatment. Then, he used any one of the chemicals mentioned, plus in-between applications of thinned hydrogen peroxide; the clinging capacity of each layer of patina was greatly increased. (I have seen such deeply incrusted objects—mostly bells—in Mexico; although I failed to uncover the "secret" of the treatment, it was obvious that only etching, that is pre-corroding of the surface, could have produced such surface roughness.)

After finishing this part of the treatment, the well patined object was placed in a mud bath—common soil and water—and subsequently heated to the boiling point. In this way, not only were all the crystalline residues of acids removed, but a sensational effect was achieved: the fine mud penetrated the minute surface pores and settled deep in the patina. Then followed drying, rinsing in clear water, drying again, and polishing with linseed oil. The objects were polished dry and cleaned only superficially with a brush. This treatment actually produced an appearance of age-old dirt. It looked as if the object had been secreted for centuries in a closed room untouched by dirt—perhaps a tomb—wherein it had been "found."

Mr. Domes closes his account by stating that the cold processes he describes have one great advantage—you can use them on top of a genuine old patina without ruining it. In this manner, a defective patina can be corrected and valuable pieces can be saved. This fact alone gives one the right to expose the secrets of the forgers and imitators; the information is not meant to encourage those "professionals" who produce "antique" relics, but to aid responsible conservators.

And the same, I might add, applies to many disciplines discussed in this manual— all are designed either to restore what time and circumstance may have destroyed, or to recreate appearances that would delight our senses.

Treatment of pewter

All one can do with antique pewter objects is to clean them. Special compounds suitable for this purpose are commercially available. A paste made of linseed oil and rottenstone will also work very well as a cleansing agent. The paste should be placed on a rag and rubbed into the surface of the object. It can then be washed off with soap and water. There does not seem to be any satisfactory method of patining modern pewter. As with all metals, oxidation can be prevented by a protective coat of Krylon spray or wax-resin compound.

Treatment of iron

Nothing could be simpler than giving new iron the appearance of age. Dipping it alternately in sulphuric and muriatic acid and heating it with the torch or Bunsen burner will produce the desired result at once. For the removal of rust, one can use a commercial rust solvent; prolonged immersion in a 10% solution of oxalic acid, aided by some rubbing, will also be effective.

7
RESTORING PAINTINGS

Comparatively few books have appeared on restoring paintings and these have rarely proven helpful to the non-specialist. True, some competent restorers have, on rare occasions, disclosed certain of their own practices; but other practitioners have approached the subject with an apparatus so complex that only someone who has served his apprenticeship in a restorer's shop—and possesses elaborate equipment—could possibly profit by these written instructions. In this chapter, I shall describe a few simple methods of picture restoration that can be carried out by any painter—methods based on specific case histories.

But let me remind you of the warning at the opening of this book. No matter how simple and foolproof a procedure may be, I would not advise anyone who is inexperienced to try his hand on a painting of obvious value. Unless you are quite familiar with the problem at hand, restoration of valuable works of art should be left to a qualified specialist.

Cleaning paintings

First, I should like to emphasize that no generally valid rules can be established. Means used for cleaning pictures may cover a wide range: superficial dusting; sponging with soap and water; employing half a dozen chemicals; even scraping a picture's surface with a knife when necessary. We shall start with the simplest operations and then progress to more complex procedures.

Superficial cleaning

If the problem is simply superficial dirt—commonly deposited by polluted city air—here is a direct, uncomplicated procedure.

Accumulated dust should be removed from the surface with a soft, dry cloth. After wiping off the loose dust, the more tenaciously clinging dirt can be removed by rubbing the paint surface with one's fingers. Repeated "massaging"—and intermediate hand washing—will relieve the paint texture of most, and sometimes all, of the clinging impurities.

Next, a wad of surgical cotton or cheesecloth should be saturated with damar picture varnish or copal varnish (the Permanent Pigments formula) and gently rubbed into the surface. This will amount to cleaning and revarnishing in one operation.

A note of caution: apply this varnish without undue pressure. If a paint film is less than one year old, care should be taken not to soften its surface by the action of the turpentine contained in the varnish. Furthermore, paint that is weakly bound to the surface will begin to come off. This will become evident at once by any discoloration of the cotton used for rubbing. If this happens, substitute copal painting medium (Permanent Pigments) for the varnish and apply carefully with a soft brush or fingertips. Cheesecloth will exert greater pressure on the surface; hence this material should be used only on older paintings.

Cleaning with soap and water

If the dirt is too tenacious for the "finger method," recent paintings in good condition may be subjected to cleaning with mild soap and water applied by a moist cloth or a sponge. "Good condition" means that the paint film does not show cracks, breaks, or openings through which moisture could penetrate to the reverse side. Holding a canvas against strong light will reveal whether the paint film admits light, although when dealing with a heavy linen fabric, this may not be conclusive evidence. The surface of older paintings should be examined with a magnifying glass.

Should moisture reach the linen, it would make the fibers swell and then, upon drying, they would shrink. Thus, the fabric would be subjected to considerable movement which a thoroughly dry paint film (on an old picture) will not be able to follow. In consequence, a well dried picture may develop a net of cracks and flake off in spots. However, a relatively fresh (that is, only a few years old) paint film will not suffer from such movement.

When cleaning a painting with soap and water, the sponge or cloth used for this purpose should be moist—not wet. Every trace of soap (which will later absorb water) should be carefully removed when the cleaning is completed. When the surface is thoroughly dry, varnish with damar picture varnish. This can be done with a brush or with a piece of cheesecloth, which is much easier. Spraying the varnish from a pressure can is entirely inappropriate because a sprayed film does not conform to the configurations of the paint texture.

Cleaning with strong solvents

For even more tenacious surface films, a stronger solvent than soap is saponin, a white powder obtained from certain plants such as soapwort. It is soluble in water, in which it foams like soap. Like soap, it will not remove a varnish film, but some stains deposited by the air on the painting—such as impurities contained in tobacco smoke and kitchen fumes—although they resist soap, will yield to saponin. A teaspoonful of the powder should be dissolved in about 4 oz. of warm water. A small addition of ammonia will considerably strengthen its action; hence it should be used with great care and only on old, thoroughly dry pictures.

Solvents that will remove various varnishes, dirt, and later overpaints are, in order of their strength: acetone, the strongest, miscible with water, oil, and petroleum derivatives, hence a useful coupling agent for combining immiscible fluids; methanol (denatured alcohol); xylol or toluol (coal tar derivatives); turpentine; and mineral spirits, the weakest and therefore least likely to dissolve a delicate paint film.

Which of these solvents would be appropriate for a particular painting? Actual tests must be conducted at the edges of paintings that are to be cleaned. Century old paintings may have been subjected to improper varnishing and various methods of "rejuvenation" at one time or another. These methods are often beyond our calculation. Drying and non-drying oils, floor varnishes, shellac, and still more outlandish substances may have left a skin that can defy all known solvents and make the restorer resort to the use of a knife for a laborious scraping of the surface inch by inch—an attack which I do not recommend to the inexperienced reader.

Brief case histories of cleaning

To give the reader a general idea of some typical circumstances which I have encountered in cleaning paintings, here are a few examples:

(1) A painting several years old, covered by dust while in storage, was dusted with a soft cloth, rubbed with the fingertips, and wiped with a moist cloth.

(2) A painting about fifteen years old was superficially dusted. A sponge was dipped in soapy water and all excess water was squeezed out. After sponging the surface and freeing it from the soapy residue with a clean, slightly moist sponge, I then dried it with a soft cloth.

(3) A painting twenty years old, obscured by a yellow film, evidently due to tobacco smoke and/or kitchen fumes, was treated with saponin solution (after dusting as indicated above) using cheesecloth. Upon drying, I rubbed the surface gently with a piece of surgical cotton dipped in xylene, thus removing the old varnish and some dirt incorporated in the varnish film.

(4) An early 19th century painting had been covered with a dark orange film of varnish that almost completely obscured its surface. Only methanol proved to be effective in this case. It removed the coating instantaneously. The alcohol obviously worked so well because the orange coating must have been shellac.

(5) On a completely darkened, deep brown 18th century American painting, acetone, our strongest solvent, was tried without success. Next, the surface was subjected to the action of saponin with a little concentrated ammonia added. This solvent cleaned the painting speedily and completely, removing what must have been an accumulation of grime, tobacco smoke, and other impurities.

(6) An 18th century painting considerably darkened and yellowed, probably due to an oil-resin varnish coating, was cleaned of its obscuring film with a mixture of equal parts of alcohol (methanol) and toluene. As you rub the surface of a painting with cheesecloth or surgical cotton, be sure to examine it frequently to see whether it has picked up dirt or color. Should color start to come off conspicuously, the solvent used should be neutralized at once with a restraining agent; the action of saponin, alcohol, and acetone can be stopped with water.

Repairing bulges

One common damage to canvas is a bulge caused by an object pressed against the picture. On relatively fresh paintings, even a major bulge—providing that it does not occur in an area of a considerable impasto (thick paint)—may not show a break in the paint. To rectify such a bulge, the reverse side of the canvas should be slightly moistened (not made wet) and the stretchers should be tightened by means of keys (Fig. 78) to make the canvas taut.

In severe cases, where minor fissures appear in the paint on the area of the bulge, the picture should be placed face down on a clean table. Next, after moistening the reverse side of the affected part, a few sheets of blotting paper should be placed on the moistened area and pressed down with a heavy weight (a stack of books weighing at least 30 lb. can be used for this purpose). The canvas should remain under pressure for twelve hours or longer. Should this measure prove ineffective, the application of a patch or a complete relining will be required, as described later in this chapter.

FIGURE 78. *Wooden keys (secured by nails) in corners of stretcher bars keep canvas taut.*

Removing creases

Creases caused by the pressure of the underlying stretcher bars, unless the deformity is superficial and occurs on a relatively new painting, may not respond to simply moistening the canvas—although this should be tried first. If this fails, the canvas should be taken off the stretchers; the area around the crease should be slightly moistened at the back and then pressed with a warm (not hot!) laundry iron. This should be done on the reverse side of the picture with a sheet of newspaper between canvas and iron.

Superficial creases will disappear after this treatment. However, on old painting's, particularly along the edges of the stretcher bars, the paint will often crack, in which case only relining (described later in this chapter) will remedy the condition.

Causes of cracks

Cracks caused by pressure against the canvas are the most common damage seen on old paintings; these flaws, if extensive, must be

FIGURE 79. *Aluminum plate with wooden support was constructed by author to slide between stretchers and canvas, thereby providing firm base for repairs.*

dealt with by relining. Let us now examine the nature and character of these defects.

I mentioned pressure against the canvas. Are there any other reasons why a paint surface may crack? Indeed, some cracks occur because of faulty painting technique. Others occur "normally" due to the process of aging.

We must consider that a canvas is always hygroscopic (it absorbs moisture) and thus it will react to changes in atmospheric moisture, expanding at high and contracting at low humidity. Consequently, an old canvas —a century old or even more—will acquire a fine network of cracks because a dry paint film cannot follow the expanding and contracting movements of its support. Such slight crackle does not deface the surface appearance of a painting, and relining can make the cracks almost invisible. It is also normal for an old paint stratum to show a loss of paint body, in other words, shrinkage; cracks due to this circumstance are more conspicuous than the former, and cannot be rectified entirely through relining.

Cracks resulting from faulty technique or the use of inferior materials are not evident in "old masters," but are quite common in some late 18th and particularly 19th century paintings. These often appear as wide open gaps with a characteristic design reminiscent of alligator skin, hence this phenomenon is called "alligatoring." Defects of this nature can be corrected only by heavy overpainting. Relining will be of no avail here.

Now let us look at the nature of cracks due to other than internal causes. Cracks in old pictures may involve the entire thickness of the paint strata as well as the priming (the white undercoat) and even the sizing (the glue that is applied to the raw canvas beneath the priming). "Old pictures" need not necessarily be centuries old; a painting left near a furnace, or in a storage area where the relative humidity may stand at 10% or less, will age more in one year than it would in fifty years if kept in an environment where the average relative humidity registers 45%. Cracks may appear on such a canvas at points of greatest stress: at the corners (these cracks will run diagonally to a corner), or at the periphery, where short cracks will run at right angles to the stretcher bar. The only remedy here is relining. If you lack proper equipment, home relining of large paintings may not be feasible. In such cases, you would have to remove the entire cracked area, down to the bare canvas. This sounds ominous but the procedure is rather simple.

Removing and repainting a cracked area

Step by step, the procedure is this.

(1) Dissolve the affected paint areas with a commercial paint remover; this will be done effortlessly. The priming, however, is anchored to the grain of the sized canvas and will offer greater resistance. After softening it with paint remover, scrape off the priming with a scraper (Fig. 35).

(2) The residue of paraffin, which the paint remover has left on the surface, should be eliminated with turpentine. Then the glue size that remains on the raw canvas should be softened with warm water.

(3) The cleaned area of the canvas should finally be pressed flat with a warm laundry iron.

The entire operation should be carried out on top of the home made contraption shown in Fig. 79. It is made of a cross-like wooden support (with two depressions to serve as a handle) on which rests a thin but inflexible aluminum plate that extends

2″ all around—exactly the width of the stretcher bars. Thus, this metal part can be inserted between the stretchers and the canvas (should the damage appear in that area), lending the affected canvas a firm support.

(4) Now the cleaned and smoothly pressed canvas should be sized and primed. But instead of glue size and white lead priming (the traditional materials used for preparing canvas), we shall use acrylic gesso only because, unlike the glue, it will not exert an undue pull on the canvas as it dries. When the first gesso application dries, it should be sandpapered. Then a second gesso application and perhaps a third priming (which can be white lead) should follow to approximate the thickness of the original priming.

(5) Next, one can proceed with underpainting, overpainting, or whatever manipulations might have gone into the painting of the original picture.

Patching damaged canvases

Smaller, less significant cracks, appearing on a few isolated spots, can be patched up—should one wish to avoid relining or the radical procedure just described. The linen used for patching should be very smooth; it should be cut 1″ larger all around than the cracked area to be patched. The central area of the patch should be covered with adhesive—acrylic medium—stopping short of the edges of the patch, and leaving a 1″ border free of adhesive. This will prevent the edges of the patch from digging into the canvas when pressure is later applied. The reverse side of the patched area of the canvas should also be covered with the adhesive and the patch applied, again being careful that the borders of the patch are left free. Patch and canvas are now pressed with a not-too-hot laundry iron.

Next, insert two or three layers of newspaper between the 1″ borders of the patch (which are not glued down) and the canvas, again to prevent the edges of the patch from being impressed upon the picture when pressure is applied. Place several layers of newspaper over the patch, and set a piece of Masonite on top, weighed down with one or two cinderblocks (two if the cracks are deep). The sheets of newspaper should be larger than the Masonite board; this is necessary to prevent the edges of the board from being impressed into the picture. The picture should be left in this improvised press for twenty-four hours.

Loss of paint

Poor adhesion is responsible for paint flaking off a canvas in spots, forming cavities called "lacunae." These should be filled with a putty traditionally prepared from white lead oil paint (flake white), with some color added. It is best to make this putty match the color to be replaced. But whatever that color may be, some umber oil paint should be mixed with it to accelerate drying; depending on the thickness of the paint, drying may take a day or even several days. The putty should be spread into the lacuna with a painting knife, and the level of the filled area kept just below the level of the surrounding color, thus leaving room for corrective painting.

Tears

A tear in a canvas, most frequently concommitant with a loss of paint around the torn area, can be repaired successfully by patching or relining, and subsequent filling of the lacuna. If the damaged area carries a heavy impasto, you *may* cover the tear by patching or relining, plus a subsequent heavy overpainting. In most cases, however, re-

weaving of the linen fabric is imperative. Obviously, such work requires artful mending and this cannot be carried out by the inexperienced; it should always be entrusted to the specialist. Once the fabric has been repaired, priming with acrylic gesso, filling with flake white putty, or underpainting can precede the final overpainting.

I shall repeat once more why I recommend priming with acrylic gesso—instead of sizing with glue and then priming with white lead, the traditional way of preparing a canvas for oil painting. Glue size, if used on isolated spots, has a tendency to pull as it dries, thus forming folds that radiate all around the sized area. This is not the case with acrylic gesso, which can be applied directly to the canvas without prior sizing.

Relining on panels

Thus far, I have discussed "makeshift" repairs that can be done by those who may shun a complete job of relining—which means attaching the painting to a fresh surface. True, after reading the descriptions of procedures in any of the existing manuals, with their complex recipes and apparatus—the layman may not venture to attempt relining at all. However, now that we have the polyvinyl acetate adhesive known commercially as white glue, the process has become quite simple.

For relining small paintings (up to about 12″ x 16″) I would suggest a rigid support, such as a Masonite panel. I realize that some authorities would look askance upon this recommendation. Indeed, a trained eye will discover a certain rigidity on a canvas relined in this manner; this is particularly conspicuous on larger pictures. But pictures relined on linen also show a certain surface stiffness. To add to the confusion, we often find this process carried out in reverse on many important works of the 15th and 16th century, originally done on wood panels and then transferred to canvas because the original support had deteriorated. To the attentive observer, the incongruous surface appearance of such paintings is quite obvious. Hence, to maintain a strict orthodoxy in this matter does not appear to be reasonable. At any rate, when relining small paintings, we shall have no compunction in using Masonite panels for their support, especially when we consider that this will safeguard a picture from future damage.

Relining on a panel is very simple. Untempered Masonite, $\frac{1}{8}$" thick, is the appropriate material. For fine fabrics, use the smooth side of the board; which carries a textured surface. Whichever side is chosen, it should first be made nonabsorbent by covering it with acrylic gel medium. Now here are the steps in relining.

(1) After taking the old, damaged canvas off the stretchers, it should be trimmed at the edge where it folds over the stretcher bars. The reverse side of the canvas should be well smoothed with sandpaper; an electric sander is most useful for this purpose. This operation is important because the canvas will be subjected to pressure and its fibers—especially the small knots—will impress themselves on the painted surface.

(2) This done, apply the white glue generously with a spatula. Press the adhesive firmly into the fibers of the fabric. The damaged areas should be well saturated with the liquid. The panel should also be covered by the adhesive.

(3) Place the picture on the panel while the glue on both surfaces is still wet. Cover the painting with a few sheets of newspaper and press with a not-too-hot laundry iron. The object here is to soften the paint slightly under the heat, but not enough to make the paper stick to the paint. (Should this

happen, rub the paper off with your moistened finger.) All the areas that show cracks should be well pressed out. The picture should be cleansed of all traces of adhesive that may have penetrated to the paint surface; use a damp cloth or rub the glue off with your fingers.

(4) The picture should now be placed face up on a larger Masonite panel (on the floor or on a table) and covered again with sheets of newspaper. Place another Masonite panel on top and weigh the whole down with cinderblocks. (One cinderblock weighs 35 lbs.; in case these are not available, you can use any object of approximate weight.) Because the evaporation of the liquid adhesive is very slow in the almost airtight press, the relined painting should remain under pressure for at least twenty-four hours, preferably longer. However, the newspaper which covers the painting absorbs moisture from the adhesive; therefore, the paper should be replaced several times during the drying period. Cracks appearing on light paint surfaces may have accumulated dust; after relining they will appear as fine dark hairlines on the painting and these may be retouched.

Relining on canvas

Relining on canvas is not as simple as on a panel (Figs. 80-83), although the process is almost identical. The canvas chosen for this purpose should be the primed cotton duck used for painting. Its unprimed side will be used for attaching the old canvas.

(1) The picture should be taken off the stretchers, trimmed at the edge where it folds over the stretcher bars, and its reverse side well sandpapered. The canvas used for relining should be cut 1" larger all around than the picture to be attached.

(2) Place the trimmed picture on the

FIGURE 80. *Badly cracked corner of painting, due to pressure of object against canvas.*

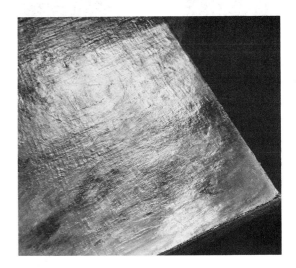

FIGURE 81. *Same canvas after relining, some retouching. Cracks have disappeared.*

FIGURE 82. *Sharp, parallel cracks caused by internal stress due to desiccation.*

FIGURE 83. *Cracks in the surface have disappeared after relining.*

sheet of new canvas and mark the outlines of the old canvas on the new with a piece of charcoal. On the reverse side of the new support, mark with charcoal all the areas of the painting that show cracks, since these will require an especially thorough pressing with a laundry iron.

(3) Use a spatula to cover the reverse side of the old picture and the surface of the new support with white glue; but leave a 1" border free of adhesive on the new support. Later, this edge will be folded over the stretcher bars and nailed on. Now place the picture on the new support, cover it with newspaper, and commence pressing the surface as you did on the panel. Your laundry iron should not be too hot! Work over the cracked areas with vigor. Of course, when working directly on the paint film, great care must be taken not to overheat it.

(4) Clean away the adhesive that may have penetrated to the surface. Reverse the picture, protect the surface with newspaper, and press the back with the iron.

(5) Next comes the press. Protected by newspaper on both sides and held between two Masonite panels, the picture should be subjected to twice the weight used on the rigid panel support. After about ten hours, the protecting paper (which will now feel moist) can be replaced, and then replaced again the next day. The picture should be left in the press for about two days.

(6) Take it out of the press, nail it onto the stretchers at once, and make the canvas taut by means of the keys, which should be safely secured in their position with nails (Fig. 78). The canvas is still slightly moist; stretching it would not be as easy after all moisture has evaporated from the fabric.

Retouching

All necessary retouching should be done on a relined painting after varnishing. The reason for varnishing prior to retouching is this: more often than not, flat or dull spots will crop up on the relined canvas and thus obscure its true appearance. Varnishing will eliminate these spots, restore a unified surface, and make retouching easier.

After varnishing, but before retouching, some copal painting medium (Permanent Pigments) should be rubbed onto the varnished surface. When dealing with old and valuable paintings, the painting medium should be relatively impermanent; it should, when necessary for future restoration, yield easily to a mild solvent. A mixture of damar varnish and linseed oil, in equal proportions, should be used.

How much license can one take in replacing lost paint? Consider: most of the paintings you see in museums have been "doctored" to a lesser or larger extent—although these facts are not advertised by museum officials. Fortunately, because these additions were generally executed with an impermanent medium, they can be removed at any time should this appear desirable. (See restoration sequence in Figs. 84-86.)

Preventing mold

When you are dealing with old (or not so old) paintings, the presence of mold should be considered. As we know, glue is used for sizing canvas; prolonged high humidity and warm temperatures will often produce mold. Its prevention or elimination is simple. Spray the back of the picture lightly with a 5% solution of thymol in methanol; or touch up the affected parts with a piece of cloth moistened with a 40% solution of formaldehyde.

Revarnishing paintings

Paintings should not be varnished directly

after they have been cleaned because their linoxyn (dried paint film) may have small fissures and cracks that have allowed the volatile cleaning agent to penetrate to the reverse side of the canvas. If they are not given time to evaporate, such solvents will destroy the cohesiveness of varnish films. Hence, one should start varnishing twenty-four hours after cleaning.

On a well hardened painting surface, the use of copal varnish is most appropriate. On a fresh, still relatively soft paint film, damar retouching varnish will provide protection until the surface is well hardened.

I must caution the reader that the term "copal" may mean anything and varnish formulations vary greatly; for this reason, I am referring specifically to the product that carries my name and is manufactured by Permanent Pigments of Cincinnati, Ohio. This hard resin varnish is much more resistant to atmospheric attacks than any of the soft resins, such as mastic and damar; but because copal varnish is compounded in a thin, volatile solution, it can be removed without much effort. Copal is recommended only for well hardened surfaces because it is obviously futile to apply a permanent varnish to a fresh surface which is still undergoing chemical change which will destroy the varnish coat.

The "ideal" protection calls first for the application of copal varnish and, after a few days, another application of the weaker damar picture varnish. Thus, if the time comes when the soft top varnish has become dirty and thus obscures the painting, it can be removed while the underlying protective film of tougher copal varnish will remain intact.

The varnish film should cover the paint surface sparingly; the thinnest film can be obtained by applying the varnish with cheesecloth. Should one wish to super-

FIGURE 84. *Baroque (18th century) canvas shows cracks, wrinkles, loss of paint, dirty surface before treatment.*

FIGURE 85. *Same painting after relining, partial cleaning, shows paint loss where original paint was loose, brittle.*

FIGURE 86. *Painting fully cleaned, earlier retouchings removed, gaps filled and overpainted, discolorations retouched, surface varnished.*

impose damar picture varnish on top of copal, only a brush should be used, so as not to rub away the underlying varnish film. Only a small area, about 10″ square, should be varnished at a time. Even when I use a brush, I rub the still wet surface with the side of my hand to press the liquid into the paint configuration. To observe the spreading of the liquid, the canvas should be held at a slant toward the window. Held in such a position, the canvas will show which areas are glossy and which are dull.

Of course, a varnished painting will be glossy, but gloss in an old painting is unavoidable, for a flat, non-glossy paint film will not allow the true color to reveal itself. However, there is a way of making the gloss less conspicuous by using a product such as matte picture varnish (Permanent Pigments). This varnish, which must be applied with a brush rather than a cloth (to avoid buffing), will produce a satiny surface largely free from disturbing glare.

Waxing panels

A very durable finish can be applied to paintings done on panels (and also on canvas) with wax-resin compound. Because considerable pressure must be exerted to spread the wax, the support reproduced in Fig. 69 should be used when working on a canvas. Spreading should be done with one's fingers; buffing can follow hours later, allowing time for the turpentine to evaporate.

A word on synthetic varnishes. These are reliable on all counts, but their substance does not seem to be homogeneous with the substance of the paint film. Moreover, they come in spray cans, and spraying varnishes is entirely inappropriate. As I have previously said, a sprayed varnish film does not conform to the configurations of the paint surface. Moreover, to produce a cohesive film, an excessive quantity of varnish would have to be sprayed on. This surplus will collect in pools on the picture's surface, especially in the recesses of the paint texture, creating unpleasant effects. Thus, despite their chemical reliability, synthetic spray varnishes are to be avoided.

8
NOTES ON MATERIALS, EQUIPMENT, SOURCES OF SUPPLY

The following sources of supply will provide most of the materials and equipment required in this book—beyond those items normally found in your local paint store, hardware store, etc.

Art materials. Mail order catalogs are available from Arthur Brown & Bro., Inc., 2 West 46th Street, New York, N.Y. 10036; A. I. Friedman, Inc., 25 West 45th Street, New York, N.Y. 10036; Permanent Pigments, Inc., 2700 Highland Avenue, Cincinnati, Ohio 45212.

Chemicals. City Chemical Corp., 132 West 22nd Street, New York, N.Y. 10011.

Wood finishing materials. H. Behlen & Bro., 10 Christopher Street, New York, N.Y. 10014.

Woodworking and metalworking tools and materials. Allcraft Tool & Supply Co., Inc., 15 West 45th Street, New York, N.Y. 10036.

Now for some general notes on materials, tools, and other items that may or may not be familiar to the reader.

Abrasives. See *pumice, rottenstone, sandpaper, steel wool.*

Abrasol. Liquid for leveling areas of wood repaired with *burn-in sticks.* H. Behlen & Bro. Chapter 2.

Acetic acid. Highly corrosive liquid for patining metals. City Chemical Corp. or local chemical supplier. Chapter 6.

Acetone. Highly volatile solvent for cleaning paintings. Also dissolves acrylics. Drug stores. Chapter 7.

Acids. For patining metals. City Chemical Corp. or local chemical supplier. Chapter 6.

Acrylic artists colors. Synthetic (plastic) paints available in tubes, jars, squeeze bottles. Water soluble when wet, water insoluble when dry, except in acetone, lacquer thinner. Liquitex brand recommended. Art material stores.

Acrylic colors. See *acrylic artists colors.*

Acrylic gel medium. Adhesive for gilding, sealer for wood. Same as *acrylic painting medium,* but in gel form. Liquitex brand recommended. Art material stores. Chapter 3.

Acrylic gesso. Synthetic (plastic) *gesso* for surfacing wood, priming canvas. Liquitex brand recommended. Chapter 1.

Acrylic medium. See *acrylic gel medium, acrylic painting medium, matte acrylic medium.*

Acrylic modeling paste. Combination of *acrylic painting medium,* marble dust for repairing wood, stone, etc. Liquitex brand recommended. Art material stores. Chapters 1, 4, 5.

Acrylic painting medium. For use in mixtures with *dry pigments* (for coloring wood and other materials), as an adhesive, as a protective coating. Dries glossy, water insoluble. See *matte acrylic medium.* Liquitex brand recommended. Art material stores. Chapters 1, 3, 4, 5.

Acrylic polymer medium. See *acrylic gel medium, acrylic painting medium, matte acrylic medium.*

Aerosol spray paints. Paint, hardware, art material stores. *Krylon* and H. Behlen & Bro. products recommended. Chapter 2.

Agate burnishers. See *burnishers.*

Alcohol. See *denatured alcohol, shellac thinner.*

Alcohol soluble dyes. For coloring *shellac* and repairing cracks in wood. H. Behlen & Bro. Chapters 1, 3.

Aluminum leaf. Substitute for *silver leaf.* Larger art supply stores and H. Behlen & Bro. Chapter 3.

Ammonia water (concentrated 28%). Added to *saponin,* used for cleaning paintings. Used alone for softening shellac hardened brushes, patining metals. (Do not use household ammonia.) Drug stores. Chapters 6, 7.

Ammonium butyrate, carbonate, chloride, nitrate, sulphate. For patining metals. Dilute with water at least 1:4. Local chemical supplier or City Chemical Corp. Chapter 6.

Aniline dyes. For coloring wood. See *dyes, alcohol soluble dyes.* H. Behlen & Bro. Chapter 1.

Aquatint. A method of coating metal with partially melted granules of rosin dust and etching with acid. Chapter 6.

Artists oil colors. Art material stores.

Asphaltum. Dissolved in *turpentine,* used for coloring gilding, and creating crackled surfaces. Larger art supply stores and H. Behlen & Bro. Chapters 2, 3, 4.

Beeswax (bleached or unbleached). Dissolved in *turpentine* (1:3) to make wax paste for finishing, preserving, coloring wood. Dissolved in *copal* or *damar varnish* to make *wax-resin compound,* it serves the same purposes, but is superior to the wax-turpentine mixture. Unprocessed wax is available in drugstores. Chapter 1.

Behloid Satin Dull Table Top. Wood varnish produced by H. Behlen & Bro. Chapter 2.

Benzene. Solvent for oils and varnishes, used in cleaning paintings. Local chemical supplier or City Chemical Corp. Chapter 7.

Bleach Booster. For bleaching wood. H.

Behlen & Bro. Chapter 1.

Bristle brushes. Art material stores.

Bunsen burner. Gas burner with open flame that can be regulated. Scientific supply houses and some hardware stores. Chapter 1.

Burn-in sticks. Meltable colored sticks for filling cracks and nicks in finished wood surfaces. H. Behlen & Bro. Chapter 2.

Burnishers. For polishing gold, silver leaf, and *acrylic modeling paste.* Agate burnishers are best, but those made of steel are also usable. Larger art material stores or H. Behlen & Bro. Chapter 3.

Calcium chloride. For patining metals. Dilute with water at least 1:4. Local chemical supplier or City Chemical Corp. Chapter 6.

Carbolic acid. Also called *phenol.* Germicide to preserve *gum arabic, glue size,* etc. Drug stores.

Carbon tetrachloride. Non-flammable solvent for oils, soft resins. Cleaning agent. Use in well ventilated room; toxic. Drug stores.

Carnauba wax. Hardest of all natural waxes. For making *wax-resin compound.* Local chemical supplier or H. Behlen & Bro. Chapter 1.

Cement. See *Portland cement.*

Chalk (powdered). For making white transfer paper and cleaning fingers when handling leaf. Crush common sticks of white chalk, available in stationery stores, dime stores, etc.

Cheesecloth. For cleaning and varnishing paintings, producing textures on wood surfaces. Department stores, dime stores, etc.

Clay. See *gilder's clay.*

Clorox. Common bleach for wood, cloth. Drug stores, super markets, and grocery stores, etc.

Cobalt dryer. Added to oil paint to speed drying. Art supply stores.

Color Dissolvent. For bleaching wood. H. Behlen & Bro. Chapter 1.

Copal painting medium. For restoring paintings. Combines Congo copal resin, stand oil, *linseed oil, turpentine.* Formula compounded by author produced by Permanent Pigments. Art material stores. Chapter 6.

Copal varnish. For varnishing paintings, making *wax-resin compound.* Author's formulation produced by Permanent Pigments. Art material stores. Chapters 1, 6.

Copper acetate, carbonate, chloride, nitrate, sulphate. For patining metals. Dilute with water at least 1:4. Chemical supplier or City Chemical Corp. Chapter 6.

Crackle Finish. For producing artificially aged surface on wood. Paint and hardware stores. Chapter 4.

Crude oil. Any oil used for lubricating machines. Hardware stores.

Damar varnish. For varnishing paintings, making *wax-resin compound.* See *retouching varnish.* Author's formulation produced by Permanent Pigments. Art material stores. Chapters 1, 7.

Dead Flat Finish. For finishing wood. H. Behlen & Bro. Chapter 2.

Decolorant. For bleaching wood. H. Behlen & Bro. Chapter 1.

Denatured alcohol. Also called *methanol,* methyl alcohol, *shellac thinner,* wood alcohol. For thinning *shellac,* cleaning surfaces, restoring paintings. Paint and hardware stores. Chapters 1, 7.

Detergent (or soap). Added to water based paint to prevent "crawling" when applied to surfaces of metal.

Double boiler. Also called *water bath.* Two metal vessels (usually enameled), one resting in the other. The outer vessel is filled with water which is heated on a stove or hot plate; the inner vessel contains material which is to be heated or melted, but which is not subjected to direct heat. Housewares and department stores.

Dragon's blood. Dark red resinous substance soluble in *turpentine* and hot *linseed oil.* For coloring leaf. H. Behlen & Bro. Chapter 3.

Dry pigments. For coloring wood, *wax-resin compounds;* for repairing wood, stone sculpture, etc. Larger art material stores or Fezandie & Sperrle, Inc., 103 Lafayette Street, New York, N.Y. Chapters 1, 4, 5.

Dyes. Mixed with water, alcohol for coloring wood. H. Behlen & Bro. Chapter 1.

Earth colors. Artists colors derived from minerals. Umbers, ochres, sienas, iron oxide reds, etc. Available as *acrylic artists colors, artists oil colors, dry pigments.*

Electric knife heater. For liquefying *burn-in sticks* to repair wood surfaces. H. Behlen & Bro. Chapter 2.

Electric tools. Hardware stores or Allcraft Tool & Supply Co.

Epoxy cement. Powerful plastic adhesive. Hardware stores.

Ferric nitrate, sulphate. For patining metals. Dilute with water at least 1:4. Local chemical supplier or City Chemical Corp. Chapter 6.

Flat interior paint. For finishing inexpensive furniture. Available in oil, acrylic, alkyd formulations. Paint stores. Chapter 2.

Formaldehyde. Fungicide to eliminate mold. Drug stores. Chapter 7.

Gamboge. For coloring gilding. Dissolves in *turpentine,* forming golden yellow liquid; the thicker the solution, the deeper the color. H. Behlen & Bro. Chapter 3.

Gesso. Traditional white undercoat for gilding and painting, used only on rigid surfaces (wood, *Masonite,* etc.) because of brittleness. Gesso can be made at home following instructions in Chapter 1, or can be bought in dry form in art supply stores and mixed with water. Traditional formulation contains *glue size, whiting,* water. *Acrylic gesso* is modern synthetic (plastic based) substitute. Also see *gilder's clay.* Art supply stores. Chapters 1, 3, 4.

Gilder's clay. Also called gilder's whiting. For foundations underlying *gold leaf,* etc. Especially important if leaf is to be burnished. Available in red, yellow, blue. Sold as water paste under trade name, *Heins burnishing clay.* H. Behlen & Bro. and larger art material stores. Chapter 3.

Gilder's cushion. Chamois covered pad used in cutting leaf. H. Behlen & Bro. Chapter 3.

Gilder's tip. Flat 4″ wide soft hair brush for picking up leaf. H. Behlen & Bro. Chapter 3.

Glue. Rabbit skin glue is used for making *gesso* and clay grounds for gilding, and for attaching leaf. *White glue* (plastic based) is used for mending wood and relining paintings. *Acrylic gel medium* is used for attaching leaf and sealing absorbent surfaces. *Acrylic painting medium* is used as a general purpose adhesive and protective coating. White glue is sold in hardware stores, the others at art material stores.

Glue size. For gesso, use 7% solution of *rabbit skin glue* (or hide glue) in water (1 oz. glue to 1 pt. water). For applying leaf, ½ to ¾ oz. glue in 1 pt. water. Soak overnight in water; then heat in *double boiler* to liquefy, but do not boil. Art supply stores. Chapter 1.

Gold leaf. Genuine leaf comes in book of 25 leaves, each 3⅜″ x 3⅜″. *Swift Patent Gold Leaf* is attached to underlying tissue paper for easier handling. Genuine leaf is also available in ribbons of various widths. *Metal leaf* (imitation gold) in book form measures 5½″ x 5½″. Larger art supply stores and H. Behlen & Bro. Chapter 3.

Gum Arabic. Water soluble gum mixed with *artists oil colors* to make emulsion for graffito technique and for producing *crackle finish.* Larger art supply stores and H. Behlen & Bro. Chapters 3, 4.

Heins burnishing clay. Foundation for *gold leaf.* See *gilder's clay.*

Hydraulic cement. See *Portland cement.*

Hydrochloric acid. Highly corrosive acid for patining metals. Use with care. Muriatic acid is not a substitute. Local chemical supplier or City Chemical Corp. Chapter 6.

Hydrogen peroxide. Oxidizing agent for patining metals. Drug stores. Chapter 6.

Incra Patine. For patining bronze, copper, brass. David Litter Laboratories, 116 East 16th Street, New York, N.Y. Chapter 6.

Iron chloride, sulphate. For patining metals. Iron chloride is also used for etching. Dilute with water at least 1:4. Local chemical supplier or City Chemical Corp. Chapter 6.

Japan size. For attaching leaf. Hardware and paint stores or H. Behlen & Bro. Chapter 3.

Jet-Spray Lacquer. Used as fixative and surface finish. Available in transparent form (will not produce gloss on rough or absorbent surface) as well as colors, gold, silver. H. Behlen & Bro. Chapter 2.

Krylon. Acrylic based spray available in transparent form (for fixative), colors, gold, silver. Art material stores.

Lacquers. For high gloss finishes. Hardware and paint stores or H. Behlen & Bro. Chapter 2.

Linen. Raw, unprimed linen is used for patching, relining paintings. Art material stores. Chapter 7.

Linseed oil. For polishing wood. Artists' quality is sold in art material stores, woodworkers' quality in paint, hardware stores. Chapter 1.

Liver of sulphur. Also called *potassium sulphate.* For patining metals. Dilute with water at least 1:4. Local chemical supplier or City Chemical Corp. Chapter 6.

Machine oil. Also called *crude oil.* For furniture finishing technique called French polish. Hardware stores. Chapter 1.

Masking tape. Pressure sensitive tape used to mask parts of surface which must be protected from paint, lacquer, etc. Art material stores, stationery stores, etc. Chapter 2.

Maskoid. Quick drying liquid that forms film serving same funtion as *masking tape.* Can be peeled off when dry. Art material stores. Chapter 2.

Masonite Composition board made of wood fibers. Available ⅛″ and ¼″ thick, untempered and tempered (hardened). For relining paintings. Lumber yards. Chapter 7.

Matte acrylic medium. Same as *acrylic painting medium,* but dries non-glossy. Liquitex brand recommended. Art material stores.

Matte picture varnish. For varnishing paintings when non-glossy surface is required. Permanent Pigments brand recommended. Art material stores. Chapter 7.

Mercury chloride, sulphate. For patining metals. Dilute with water at least 1:4. Local chemical supplier or City Chemical Corp. Chapter 6.

Metal leaf. See *gold leaf.*

Methanol. See *denatured alcohol, shellac thinner.*

Mineral spirits. Substitute for *turpentine,* approximating same qualities, but not as strong solvent. Hardware and paint stores.

Modeling paste. See *acrylic modeling paste.*

Muriatic acid. Impure form of *hydrochloric acid,* not a substitute.

Nitric acid. Highly corrosive acid for patining metals. Handle with care. Always add to water, never vice versa. Detrimental to health if inhaled for prolonged period. Destroys bristle, sable, nylon brushes. Local chemical supplier or City Chemical Corp. Chapter 6.

Oil colors. See *artists oil colors.*

Orange shellac. See *shellac.*

Oxalic acid. Moderately corrosive acid for removing rust from iron. Local chemical supplier or City Chemical Corp. Chapter 6.

Paint remover. Most powerful solvent for removing hardened paints, varnishes, shellac, lacquers. Contains *acetone,* lacquer solvent, *methanol, paraffin* (latter inhibits evaporation). Paint and hardware stores.

Painter's thinner. Paint diluent, substitute for *turpentine.* Paint and hardware stores.

Painting knife. See *palette knife.*

Palette knife. Also called *painting knife.* Knife with elastic steel blade for manipulating heavy paints and pastes. Art material stores.

Paraffin. Refined petroleum wax, not a substitute for *beeswax.*

Petroleum solvents. See *mineral spirits, painter's thinner.*

Phenol. Also called *carbolic acid.* Germicidal preservative for organic glues. Sold in drug stores in 10% solution; add one part phenol to 100 parts glue solution.

Pigments. See *dry pigments.*

Plaster of Paris. White powder which solidifies rapidly when mixed with water to a creamy consistency. Small addition of animal glue retards drying; slow drying quality is also commercially available. Paint and hardware stores.

Polyvinyl acetate adhesive. See *white glue.*

Portland cement. Fine powder must be mixed with sand or marble dust (from 1:1 to 1:3) before adding water to form dense paste. *Acrylic painting medium* can be substituted for water; will retard drying but increases workability. Chapter 5.

Potassium sulphate. See *liver of sulphur.*

Propane torch. Produces flame from self-contained gas fuel tank. Hardware stores.

Pumice. Abrasive powder; should be mixed with water or *crude oil.* Drug stores and H. Behlen & Bro.

Putty. See *wood putty.*

Qualarenue. For renovating cracked or alligatored wood surfaces. H. Behlen & Bro. Chapter 2.

Qualatone Solvent 710. Used with *Qualarenue.* H. Behlen & Bro. Chapter 2.

Rabbit skin glue. Best quality of animal glue. Granulated glue is soaked in water overnight, liquefied by heating in *double boiler.* Larger art material stores, hardware stores, H. Behlen & Bro.

Resin. Damar and copal resins are products of trees, while acrylic and polyvinyl acetate resins are synthetic—man made plastics. First two are used in manufacture of *damar varnish, copal varnish, copal painting medium, retouching varnish.* Synthetic resins are basis of *acrylic artists colors, white glue.*

Retouching varnish. Less concentrated form of *damar varnish* for temporary protection of paintings. Author's formulation produced by Permanent Pigments. Chapter 7.

Rockhard Finish Varnish. Acid and alcohol resistant, extremely durable, glossy, quick drying varnish for wood. H. Behlen & Co. Chapter 2.

Rosin. For etching surface of metals before patining. H. Behlen & Bro. or Fezandie & Sperrle, Inc., 103 Lafayette Street, New York, N.Y. 10013.

Rottenstone. Gray, finely divided powder, similar to dust, for antiquing. Fine abrasive for polishing when mixed with water. H. Behlen & Bro.

Sable brushes. Art material stores.

Sal ammoniac. See *ammonium chloride.*

Sandpaper. General term for abrasive papers such as flint, garnet, aluminum oxide, silicon carbide. Available in all grades ranging from super fine to extra coarse. Hardware stores and H. Behlen & Bro.

Saponin. White powder; foams like soap when dissolved in water. For cleaning paintings. H. Behlen & Bro. Chapter 7.

Scriptliner. Extra long haired round sable brush for marbling wood surfaces. Art material stores. Chapter 1.

Semi-gloss Eggshell Finish. For finishing wood when moderate gloss is desired. H. Behlen & Bro.

Shellac. For wood finishing, antiquing leaf, coloring when mixed with *alcohol soluble dyes.* Available in white and orange. Paint and hardware stores. Chapters 1, 3.

Shellac thinner. Also called *denatured alcohol.* For thinning, removing *shellac.* Paint and hardware stores.

Silver leaf. Sold in book form, each leaf measures $3\frac{3}{8}''$ x $3\frac{3}{8}''$. Larger art material stores and H. Behlen & Bro. Chapter 3.

Size. See *glue size.*

Soap. See *detergent.*

Spar varnish. Outdoor, weather resistant, high gloss varnish. Paint and hardware stores.

Spatula. Trowel shaped knife, similar to *palette knife.* Art supply stores.

Spray paints. See *aerosol spray paints.*

Steel burnishers. See *burnishers.*

Steel wool. Abrasive for wood finishing. Available in grades from extra fine to coarse. Hardware stores.

Striper. Extra long haired sable brush with chisel shaped tip. For marbling wood surfaces. Art supply stores. Chapter 1.

Sulphuric acid. Highly corrosive acid for patining and cleaning metals. Thin with water 1:10 to 1:20 for cleaning. Handle with care as noted for *nitric acid.* Local chemical supplier or City Chemical Corp. Chapter 6.

Swift Patent Gold Leaf. Attached to underlying tissue paper for easier handling and cutting. Larger art supply stores and H. Behlen & Bro. Chapter 3.

Synthetic resin spray finishes. See *Jet-Spray Lacquer, Krylon.*

Tannic acid. Mix with *iron sulphate* and water to tone wood light gray to inky black. Local chemical supplier or City Chemical Co

Thymol. 5% solution in alcohol eliminates mold from paintings. Drug stores or City Chemical Corp. Chapter 7.

Toluene, toluol. For cleaning paintings. Paint and hardware stores, local chemical supplier, or City Chemical Corp. Chapter 7.

Top 'n Bond. Slow setting *cement* mix compounded with synthetic *resins.* Lumber yards and hardware stores.

Treasure Gold Liquid Leaf. Best available imitation gold paint. Art supply stores or Connoisseur Studio, P.O. Box 7187, Louisville, Ky. 40207.

Treasure Gold Wax Gilt. For gilding. Art supply stores or Connoisseur Studio, P.O. Box 7187, Louisville, Ky. 40207.

Turpentine. Diluent for paints, varnishes; used for thinning *artists oil colors,* and for dissolving dried varnish films. Housepainter's quality available in paint and hardware stores, artist's quality in art supply stores.

Varnish. See *copal varnish, damar varnish, retouching varnish.*

Venice turpentine. Viscous, resinous substance can be added (5%) to *wax-resin compounds* to enhance working quality. Larger art material stores and H. Behlen & Bro. Chapter 1.

Vibrator. For mechanical sanding of wood surfaces. Hardware stores.

Water bath. See *double boiler.*

Wax. See *beeswax, Carnauba wax, wax-resin compounds.* Commercial grade liquid or paste wax for finishing wood can be bought in hardware stores.

Wax-resin compounds. Not available commercially; must be home made. Follow directions in Chapter 1. Most effective preservative for wood surfaces.

White glue. Synthetic (plastic) glue made of polyvinyl acetate. Paint and hardware stores.

White shellac. See *shellac.*

Whiting. White pigment used in preparing traditional *gesso.* Hardware stores. Chapter 1.

Wood alcohol. See *denatured alcohol.*

Wood putty. Also called crack filler. For repairing deep cracks in wood surfaces. For shallow cracks, *acrylic modeling paste* is preferable; it dries more slowly, can be colored more easily, and can be manipulated and shaped more effectively. Hardware stores.

X-acto knife. Multi-purpose handle with detachable blades of various shapes. Art material and hobby stores.

Xylene, Xylol. Solvent for cleaning paintings. Local chemical supplier or City Chemical Corp.

Zinc sulphate. For patining metals. Dilute with water at least 1:4. Local chemical supplier or City Chemical Corp. Chapter 6.

INDEX

Frederic Taubes is an internationally known artist, with paintings owned by twenty-seven museums, including the Metropolitan Museum of Art. Educated at the academies of Vienna and Munich, and at the Bauhaus in Weimar, Mr. Taubes has served as visiting professor of art at numerous universities in the United States and Canada, and has lectured at leading colleges in Great Britain, among them London University, Oxford University, Edinburgh College of Art and the Royal College of Art. He has written more than thirty books on painting techniques and aesthetics. For eighteen years, Mr. Taubes served as Contributing Editor to *American Artist*. He has also contributed to the *Encyclopaedia Britannica* and the *Grolier Encyclopedia*. Currently, he is the American Editor of *The Artist* magazine, where he conducts the famous "Taubes Page." An acknowledged authority on painting materials, he is the formulator of the Taubes Varnishes and Painting Media, distributed throughout the world.